Who is a Guru?

and

Other Inspiring Speeches

BY

PARAMAHAMSA
OMKARANANDA SARASWATI

MOTILAL BANARSIDASS
Bangalore • Chennai • Delhi • Kolkata
Mumbai • Patna • Pune • Varanasi

Distributed by
MOTILAL BANARSIDASS
41 U.A. Bungalow Road, Jawahar Nagar, Delhi-110 007
Tel. : 2385 1985, 2385 8335, Fax : 2385 0689
Email : mlbd@mlbd.com, Website : www.mlbd.com

ISBN : 978-81-208-3536-8

First Edition 2011

Price: ₹345

Published by
SWAMI OMKARANANDA SARASWATI CHARITABLE TRUST

Printed by
THOMSON PRESS (INDIA) LIMITED
B-315, Okhla Industrial Area, Phase-1, New Delhi-110020, India

H.D. Paramahamsa Omkarananda Saraswati

INTRODUCTION

I. About Swami Omkarananda

H.D. Paramahamsa Omkarananda Saraswati is a God-realized Saint, Mystic, Sage, Philosopher and Writer.

Already at the age of thirteen and fourteen his life was flooded with numerous spiritual experiences of the omnipresent and omniscient God. Under the dictates of these experiences, he left his home city in South India for the Himalayas, where the world-renowned Sage Sri Swami Sivananda recognized in him an embodiment of the high spirit of renunciation, profound divine wisdom, touching purity of heart, made him known as Bala Yogi, Bala Jnani, titled him as Adhyatma Kavita-Bhaskara and crowned him with Sannyasa-Diksha at the age of seventeen.

The activities of Sage and Philosopher Swami Omkarananda embrace spiritual, cultural, educational, scientific and social fields. One of the significant achievements in these fields is the unique work he has done for the upliftment of the backward regions in the hills of the Himalayan Garhwal area. In recognition of his extraordinary services he has received several prestigious honours like Mother India Award, Bharat Nirman Award and Hind Rattan Award.

The Omkarananda Ashram Himalayas at Rishikesh, set on one of the foot-hills of the Himalayas, is one of the main branches of his international Institution. It aims at the realization of educational, social, cultural and spiritual projects. Omkarananda Ashram Himalayas carries on its activities through its registered Trusts – Swami Omkarananda Dharma Samsthan, Swami Omkarananda Saraswati Charitable Trust, Omkarananda Educational Society, Omkarananda Saraswati Natya Kala Academy and other educational and cultural Institutions.

Swami Omkarananda has established 74 Institutions, among them 56 Basic- and Junior-High-Schools, Degree- and Inter-Colleges, an Institute for Management and Technology, an Institute for Indian Classical Dance and Music, several Public Libraries, etc. in the beautiful hilly regions of the Garhwal Himalayas in Uttarakhand, where education was needed most.

Many beautiful Temples have been established by Shri Swami Omkarananda Saraswati in the Garhwal area, out of which the *"Omkarananda-Kamakshi-Devi Mandir"*, in typical South-Indian style, is absolutely outstanding in its beauty and purity and constitutes a landmark in whole Uttarakhand. This Temple and other lovely Temples of Omkarananda Ashram, situated in Omkarananda Nagar, Muni-ki-Reti, Rishikesh, and other places, are a center of attraction.

Swami Omkarananda is Author of many books on the subjects of Philosophy, Spirituality and Science, and his books are available in many languages, all over the world.

This is Swami Omkarananda's Life in His own words:

"Purity is the soul of my Strength. Truth is the source of my Power. God is my Life, and I have no existence apart from Him. His Consciousness is my Light. His all-sustaining and all-creative Beauty constitutes my Joy. Prayer is my Breath and meditation forms the Bread of my life.

"All Humanity is my family. The Forces of Nature are my Friends. The Godhead in all of you is the object of my adoration. It is very difficult, almost impossible, for me to differentiate or distinguish between saints and sinners or artificially divide mankind into two groups called the good and the evil, – I find there are only gracious children of God on earth, some close to, and some a little away from, God's all-purifying and all-empowering Presence.

"Human life on earth has always presented itself to me as a school in which some occupy higher standards and some lower classes, but all are to be loved equally, honoured equally, and the hand of service is to be denied to none. The people in the lower standards will one day occupy higher classes.

"I perceive real and great Beauty wherever Goodness is self-expressive and wherever Love enriches, ennobles and exalts life. I find the essential form of Beauty wherever Virtue invests human life with dignity, grants a mastery over instinctive nature and contributes to harmony and efficiency in social relations.

"I find the Face of the valuable Beauty wherever human Intelligence is active in the use of skills and in the discovery of ways and means of conquering ignorance, poverty, suffering, disease, Nature, as a measure in the progress of the soul of Humanity.

"I have no desires, but only a few wishes, and they are the wishes for the Health, Peace, Happiness, Prosperity and spiritual Progress of all people of all lands.

"I preach to nobody, but I speak to myself. I write not to teach, but to state facts. I reason not to convince others, but to eliminate the discordant elements in thinking and in living that characterize the normal nature of a growing mankind that progresses more by the method of trial and error than by ordered reason and illumination.

"I work not for any personal objective in view, but for the Glory of God and the welfare, happiness and illumination of mankind. I labour for God's blessed children under the sun, moved by a Will that is not my own but His, and with resources that belong not

to me but to the all-creative divine Consciousness that is His.

"The human individual serves mankind best, also when he thinks good thoughts, entertains noble feelings, hates none and nothing, engages himself in useful works, wishes universal welfare, prays, meditates and communes in divine Love, with the living omnipresence of the all-perfect God.

"Nothing in me has ever responded to any form of appreciation bestowed upon any of the works that proceed from me; for, all such appreciation belongs to the invisible yet discernible owner and ruler of my energies. Since all my work, way and style of life is my silent and all-inclusive worship of the living, moving, talking Godhead, – I never wished, and will never wish, to be known, even to the very next person living with me.

"I need nothing: for, the all-responding, all-wonderful, all-knowing Godhead is the Bank of my inexhaustible Fortune, my defence army of unfailing Protection and my time-defying and all-productive Factories of Life, Love and Light.

"Pleasures of life, of society, of civilization have no attraction, no value for me; for, I live in the perpetual and self-sustaining ecstasies of the Consciousness of the Divine in dynamic action and self-expression. Yet I heartily recommend the pleasures of life, of society,

of civilization to those who have not yet found the pleasures I live in; and, also I feel drawn to draw the attention of some of them to the fact that their pleasures are rendered secure, and endure, by a background awareness of God's Presence.

"I dwell in the delights of a Mind wedded to the wisdom of God, and the joys of a Heart that is lodged in the all-absorbing Love for the supreme Beloved. Pleasures are afforded to me also by aesthetic sensibilities, artistic appreciation, philosophic perceptions, spiritual intuitions.

"The idea of being a Leader is entirely foreign to my Nature. I know myself to be a ready servant of a Humanity that seeks for the peace, the strength and the joy that come from self-control and growing moral purity, the knowledge and the illumination that are gained from culture, intellectual development, perfection and the all-blessing divine powers that result from spiritual evolution and experience."

A renowned Vedic Scholar and Editor of the International Newspaper "Hinduism Today" asked Swami Omkarananda following question:

"The Journalist of the monthly newspaper HINDUISM TODAY asked the inmates of your Ashrams to describe you. We know the descriptions of you by

them and by thousand others. We need to have a description of yourself by yourself. Who are you, Swami Omkarananda?"

This was Swami Omkarananda's answer:

"Who Am I? – Before I was born, I was. After I die, I will be. A timeless Being came from, and into, timeless Eternity. Time was formed, and time is dissolved, and I remain what I have always been, a Being with depths to which there is no beginning, and heights to which there is no end.

"Since the supreme Divinity as the Timeless Eternity and as the Time Eternity – Sadashiva Tripurasundari – is dwelling in my Heart, Life, Consciousness, and as there is no difference between That and Me and Me and That, I am dwelling in the Soul of all Gods and Goddesses, all Saints and Sages, all beings visible and invisible. And, yet I am what I am, the Transcendent Reality. If you know here on earth the greatest Sage, Saint, Guru, the greatest clairvoyant, prophet, or anyone to whom supernormal power of perception, or anyone to whom daily contact with God, is attributed – then, ask that person, who Swami Omkarananda is. He will confirm to you that the only true and correct description of Swami Omkarananda is the one he himself has given."

II. About this Book

This book contains a few selected speeches of Swami Omkarananda, out of his countless speeches and talks during Satsang for spiritual Seekers.

May this book be a source of Inspiration, Joy and divine Wisdom to all the Readers.

The Publishers

Who is a Guru?

My most heartfelt Adorations to your blessed, divine feet!

You are nothing, if not direct manifestations of the omnipresent, omnipotent, omniscient Divinity.

There is no one that is to be called as Guru unless he is rooted permanently in the experience of the infinite Truth. No one can be called a Guru unless he is rooted in the Consciousness of the absolute divine Joy, Peace, Perfection, Beauty, Freedom and infinite Truth.

Be such a Guru. This is the destiny of your life. This is the glory of your human existence here on earth. Arrive at this stage! The quintessence of the Holy Scriptures consists in the simple fact: *"I die and God lives in me."* There is no dying! The "I" disappears into the perfections of the infinite wondrous divine Consciousness. The human mind and heart and soul and consciousness are displaced by the Consciousness of the divine Being. It is no more the human individual that is seeing through the eyes of the person called Guru, but the Divine Itself. Such a person is sinless, he is uplifted above all limitations of human existence, perfectly established in the poise of the transcendent Reality. His mind is the Wisdom of God. His heart is the Love of God at operation. He is in tune with the whole creation. His speech is the speech of the Divine. His breath is the breath of the Divine. He has no existence apart from the Heart and Centre of the Divine.

He is a Devotee, he is a God-Lover, who is constantly established in the realization of the all-wondrous Being that God is. In his life unconditioned Happiness, unconditioned Peace, unconditioned Freedom are operative. There is nothing in this universe that could fulfill his existence, for his existence is united with the Perfections of the divine Being. Glory to such a person! This person's state and condition is the highest evolutionary status to which you have to rise.

It is a shame to die. That means, it is a shame to experience a phenomenon called death. There is no such thing as death for one, who is established in the Consciousness of God, the Eternal, the Immortal. He is always all-conscious, supra-conscious. He is established in Consciousness. He does not sleep. He is ever awake, ever joyous. He is face to face with the infinite wonders of God. Blessed is the life of such a person. Such a person can lead mankind towards Truth and God-experience. It is such a person that becomes the vessel for the revelations and intuitions and illuminations, embodied in the greatest scriptures of the world.

Blessed are those, that meet such persons. Blessed is the earth, which bears the presence of such persons. They are our best teachers. They condition our existence to the beatitudes of the divine nature and character. All life becomes a divine ecstasy in their presence. All life discloses in such presence its real face, the face of the divine Truth. All life assumes an infinite purpose and bears an infinite joy in the presence of such persons, such Gurus.

Any Guru, who falls short in the description hereon presented, does not deserve the name Guru. Humanity has to be critical, has to exercise the power of reason and judgement at every step of life, but a judgement, that is guided by Wisdom, Love, Devotion, Grace of God. God is pulsating everywhere within us, around us, above us, below us; everywhere He is pulsating with all the perfections of his Being.

We are sorrowless Beings. Problems of existence caused by the space-time universe and the circumstances of the human society rise and disappear like clouds leaving the sky unaffected. May there be a million clouds, but nothing touches the space, contaminates the space. Space is not air to be contaminated. Space is untouchable, it cannot be defiled. It is the subtlest principle open to our senses' experience. Subtler than the space is the Divine and resident in the space is the Divine. The eyes of the Divine are everywhere. The protecting hand of the Divine is upon your blessed heads. You are blessed. Adorations to you. Realize spiritual greatness! Do not come down! Do not descend from highest standards of existence. Material goods do not make high standards of life. It is the imperishable treasures of the heart, it is the endless and inexhaustible treasures of the luminous and all-enlightened Intelligence within us, it is these, that raise the standard of our existence.

Look at yourself always in terms of the Infinite. See with the eyes of God! See with the eyes of Wisdom! Work with Love! Be ensouled by Love! Even as you are possessed by anger, be possessed by Love. Be moved by Love, impelled by Love. Be impelled by Devotion. It is the finest emotion known to the human nature. It is the liberating emotion. It is the uplifting emotion. It is the messenger that leads us to God-experience. Devotion is a mighty power. Develop devotion. Govern your daily existence by the Wisdom of God. Talk of the Infinite. Thus purify the tongue by talking of God. Purify the ear by hearing about the glories and the nature of God. Make the place, where you dwell, a heaven on earth, a powerful heaven, a heaven, where the living God is present, where God is supremely pleased in you, where God loves to dwell with you. God dwells with those, who love Him most.

Do not come down from your infinite strength, my dear friend. You have everything necessary here and now. You live, move and have your Being in God. You are rooted in the Divine, You must grow conscious of this Reality. You have no real reason, no real intelligence, no real vision, until you recognize this Truth, that you are inseparable from the all-functioning, operative presence of the infinite God.

Gurus are mirrors to your inner spiritual greatness. Their presence uplifts you, energizes you, elevates you, brings you closer to a close accessibility to the presence of the all-loving Divinity. My adorations and prostrations to you.

Guru is one, who does not see a difference between himself and all other Beings. A man, who is governed by sensorial differences is no light, is no guide, is no wise man, is not a good contact for our daily life. He is no inspiration. He has to dwell in the nature of God and express it in life, in inner experience. He must behold God, whether he opens his eyes or closes his eyes, whether he is here or there. No matter where he is, he is directly in the Heart of God. There are all heavenly Beings present, there God dwells. This is the assurance of God Himself! This is the experience of the real Gurus, Teachers and Spiritual Masters and Saints and Sages and Mystics and Yogis and Mahatmas.

May the Grace of God flow through your blessed hearts! May the Grace and Beauty and Sweetness and Love and Wisdom and Life of God throb in your veins!

God is the only Mother of mothers, the real Mother and the Mother of all mothers. He is the Sweetness of sweetness, Tenderness of tenderness. He is the Quintessence of Compassion. He is not blind. You are blind. Yet you can become by His Grace a seeing person. Acquire this grace, grow in spirituality, evolve! You are bodiless, you are spaceless. Such is the nature of the Consciousness. Even through psychological techniques, psychological self-analysis you can arrive at this fact, that Consciousness is beyond and above the body's eating habits. Live as

Consciousness, not as a dead matter, not as a perishing body.

Live as a Consciousness, a Consciousness, that is luminous, that cannot be touched, that is subtler than the space, that cannot be cut, that cannot be burdened with daily problems, while all problems dissolve themselves, when they touch Consciousness. Consciousness is Wisdom of God, Knowledge of God, Fire of God, Light of God. Light is the nature of God. He is the supreme Light, the Light of all lights known to our experience. You are Light; that Light, Divine Light. Each of you is the Divine Light Centre! As such, I give you my adorations and prostrations.

The word Guru is fantastic, because it signifies a force, a factor that removes darkness. It is a principle of the Divine that illuminates and liberates you. That is Guru. Guru is an embodiment of infinite divine Knowledge. He liberates you from human conditions, unites you with the Heart of God, makes you divine, purely by knowledge, dynamic knowledge, divine knowledge, a knowledge which is experienced the moment you know and experience, that you are not the body but the timeless Spirit of God, indestructible, all-perfect, all-fulfilled, the fullness of Joy, the fullness of Wisdom, of all Arts and Sciences, or all forms of Joy.

The moment you know yourself as the infinite Truth, you are liberated, you are free from all limitations to which time and space condition you, to which the birth in human life conditions you, freed from the limitations of human mind and heart and will.

Knowledge is Power, Wisdom is Power. Wisdom is the Liberator. Wisdom is the eternal Life-giver. Guru gives you Wisdom. Where there is Wisdom, there is Light. The nature of Wisdom is Light, it is Knowledge, it is Consciousness. The nature of Consciousness is Light. By Light, Guru illuminates you.

Guru, the Remover of darkness, the Illuminator, the Enlightener – such a Being is in perfect Union and Communion with God.

The whole world is ensouled
by the marvellous and mighty Presence
of the Divine.
Every speck of space
is filled with the infinite Power and Glory
of the Divine.
Every atom is charged
with Its Love and Ecstasy.
Here and now
anyone can experience the Divine
in all Its perfections.

Swami Omkarananda

The Intuitive Experience of the Truth

The Intuitive Experience

Intuition is the immediate knowledge of the Absolute, obtained through the eye of wisdom, as opposed to the knowledge of the external objects derived through the exercise of the senses and the intellect. It is Truth obtained by internal apprehension, without the aid of perception or the operation of the reasoning powers. It is a direct vision and apprehension of the divine Reality underlying the manifested and the unmanifested universe.

In intuition, which is knowledge springing from within, first there is the experience of the flash of gnostic light. Thereupon the aspirant is established in his own inner Self.

As intuition is a direct supramental knowledge of the Self in the immediacy of spiritual realization, there is no process of reasoning, no functioning of intellect, no experience of sensation, here. This is an inner spiritual experience which cannot be adequately described in words. Words are merely conventional. Being imperfect, language cannot express this whole, ineffable, transcendental experience. The mind and the senses require time and space to function, but the Reality which is beyond this temporal, spatial and causal order of things, can only be grasped and apprehended by intuition. Intuition is beyond relativity.

The knowledge of the Divine would have been lost to mankind but for the intuition and revelation of the Seers and Sages. The Sage in his flights of intuition, ascends to that supramental region where he experiences the divine Reality or the Absolute; and this superconscious experience is, in its nature, very vivid, vital and vibrant. Grand, sublime and profound is this intuitive Experience-Whole. It is intensely real to the Sage.

Intuition as the Only Method of Knowing Truth

Intuition is the only method of an approach to and the experience of the divine Reality.

The ultimate source of all proofs is direct apprehension. Neither the scriptures, nor the spiritual souls, can externally offer us the intimate knowledge and experience of the Reality, which must come only through an act of the inner Self in us, that sees Itself when the mind is undisturbed, unprejudiced, silenced, made calm and pure.

Intuition is the only way by which the Absolute can be realized and experienced in all its totality and integrity. The mortal, finite, limited senses and the intellect cannot comprehend the Reality which is immortal and all-pervading.

The indwelling Soul of this material universe is pure Consciousness, which, in all its integrity, the Seers have intuited; and they have given to mankind the rich and precious Wisdom of the Self.

The realization of God is possible only through intuition. It is in intuition that everything becomes clear, all doubts vanish in toto. In contrast to mediate knowledge, intuition is immediate knowledge, direct and integral. Through intuition, the aspirant perceives the truth of things without the aid of reasoning or analysis.

Truth or Brahman is inconceivable, beyond the powers of reason, and consequently, unarguable.

Therefore, the Kathopanishad declares, *"This knowledge is not to be obtained by argument, but it is easy to understand it when taught by a teacher who beholds no difference"; "the Sages, with their body, senses and mind tranquil, realize that Truth; but when it is overwhelmed with dry reasoning, it vanishes".*

Immediate intuitive experience is the criterion of Truth, for the Sages. The mood of the modern age makes the sense-perception the only test of truth.

The age of ancient philosophy was an age of intuitional perception, an age in which intuitional experience was the guarantee of Truth. The modern period is an age of the questioning, critical and analytical spirit, an age in which the guarantee of truth is the test of sense-perception. Anything which one can perceive through one's sense-organs is accepted as the reality, and everything which the senses cannot perceive is rejected as unreliable.

Thus, many a precious factor of the ancient world cultural heritage has been rejected and set aside as superstition.

Modern mind must come to realize that, in fact, intuition and intuitive discernment form the only true touchstone of philosophy. Ultimately, the method of intuition is the only method of discerning the Truth. Without developing intuition, the intellectual remains imperfect and blind to the Truth behind the appearances. In the light of the developed intuition, all other philosophies seem to be nothing more than so many systems built on interesting table-talks, funny essays, humorous attempts in the game called "blindman's buff"!

A Comparative Study concerning the Claims of Intuition and the Limitations of Intellect

Unlike reason, intuition is that power in the higher reaches of mind which perceives the truth of things in the immediacy of experience; it is a directly apprehending power of Consciousness. Dispensing with the process of reasoning and deduction, excluding mediate knowledge, intuition brings us a knowledge which is non-inferential, non-sensuous, immediate, intimate and direct.

While reason conceptually constructs knowledge, intuition apprehends in immediacy the essence of things. Reason studies the superficies of the objects of knowledge, analyses and categorizes the external nature of things; intuition experiences the very heart and truth of things.

While reason reasons about things, speaks to us of things as they appear, intuitive knowledge grasps and experiences the very life of things, brings us an awareness of the things as they are in themselves, in their essential nature.

Intuition bestows full transcendental wisdom; intellect confers the knowledge of external objects. Intuition is infallible; intellect guesses, believes, desires. Intuition is a flash and an illumination; intellect is involved in a struggle with glimmerings of knowledge. Intuition in time becomes Eternity, intuition in space becomes Infinity; in intellect, there are the distinctions of past, present and future, space and the three dimensions length, breadth and height.

The Brittle Foundations of Rational Knowledge

The conclusions of reasoning can never be uniform; hence, reason has no sure basis. Being what it is in its strength, reason cannot upset the conclusions of dynamic spiritual philosophy which are founded on the infallible and authoritative wisdom of transcendental experience.

What one person establishes through the exercise of reason, can be refuted by another more intelligent and ingenious. Even a Sage of exceptional natural powers is refuted by other Sages of equal, or greater, intellectual calibre. What one logician endeavours to establish as perfect knowledge, is demolished by another who, in his turn, is treated alike by a third. How, therefore, can knowledge which is founded on reasoning, and whose object is not something permanently uniform, be perfect knowledge?

The Chief Characteristics of Perfect Knowledge

The mark of uniformity is characteristic of perfection in knowledge. Any thing that is permanently of one and the same nature, is acknowledged to be a true or real thing. Knowledge of the Truth, or Self-Knowledge, is termed perfect or true knowledge.

In the case of perfect knowledge a mental conflict of men's opinions is not possible. But these cognitions, or knowledge, founded on reasoning, do conflict.

Once again, how can knowledge which is founded on reasoning, and whose object is not something permanently uniform, be perfect knowledge?

The Indispensability of the Intuitive Function with Regard to Matters Transcendental

Logic has no fixity, or finality. Owing to the difference of the brains of men, their reasoning powers are also different. The deductions of one reasoner are overthrown by another. We see how arguments which some clever men had cogitated with great pains are shown by people still more ingenious, to be fallacious, and how the arguments of the latter again are refuted, in their turn, by yet others. Hence, it is impossible to accept mere reasoning as having a sure foundation, on account of the diversity of men's opinions. Even if there is to be any finality of reasoning, it will not bring about any finality of doctrine in regard to the Soul, or the Truth, because the Soul, or the Truth, cannot be experienced by the senses, and neither analogy nor syllogism can apply to it.

The intellect is finite and frail, conditioned in time, space and causation; it cannot know things which are transcendental. Intellect cannot work when there is delirium, fear, disease, or the influence of some intoxication.

In matters transcendental, such as the existence of the divine Reality, of an after-life, of final release, and so on, the pronouncements of human intellect can never be perfectly free from doubt, because these are matters not within the scope of intellect. They stand beyond its scope.

Though intuition transcends reason, it is not opposed to reason.

Reason can give us only conceptual knowledge, and conceptual knowledge does not present us the knowledge of the Reality in its entirety; it divides, fragments and breaks things into pieces.

Intuitional Knowledge and Freedom from the Barriers of Human Consciousness

Since the intellect which is the seat of logical conclusions, functions on the wrong basis of the assumption that the results achieved by the process of the distinction of the knower, the knowledge and the known, are supremely trustworthy, it carries its own defects. There is no logic without this distinction of the knower, the knowledge and the known; and with this distinction, there is no eternal truth.

The complete synthesis of knowledge would be a union where reason is transcended altogether, where the intellect is wholly surpassed and differences and distinctions cancelled. This is not possible as long as the seeker rests in the human consciousness. But the practical moral urge points to the existence of perfection which is unlimited in every way, and this urge is corroborated by direct intuitive experience. It is heard from such sources that the supreme Reality is free from the functions of thinking, the notion of individuality and the perception of external existence. It is all unlimited, spaceless, timeless, non-dual, pure Consciousness. It is called Superconsciousness – for, it is greater than the ordinary consciousness experienced in life.

This does not contradict pure reason, and since reason has nothing better to say, it has to accept the trustworthy character of what is heard from those who have reached the kernel of existence. Logic may scrutinize, reason may verify the validity of these declarations; and since they are found to be agreeable to logic and reason, and as they also ratify the practical moral urge, they have to be taken as the torch in the quest after the Truth.

The Nature of the Upward Movement of Consciousness in the Phenomenon of Intuition

Pure reason takes the aspirant to the door of intuition. Intuition does not contradict reason, but surpasses it. The eye of intuition opens when the heart is purified through the practice of various spiritual disciplines, when the mind, intellect, and the senses stop their functioning. Sanjaya had this eye of intuition through the grace of Sri Vyasa. Arjuna also had the eye of intuition through the grace of Lord Krishna, and experienced Viśvarūpa-Darśana.

Intuition is the eye of wisdom; intellect is the eye of worldly knowledge. The Brahmākāra-Vṛtti that proceeds from the pure mind, or the higher mind, pertains to intuition. In intuition, the consciousness moves upwards, towards the Self and its illumination. In intellect, the common sense moves downwards to the world of illusory objects.

Types of Intuition – The Difference Between the Intuitive Perception Developed by the Disciplines of Spiritual Science, and Certain Lower Forms of Intuition

There are certain lower forms of intuition; but, in fact,

they cannot be ranked with intuition as such. The creative power of the unconscious mind is such that sometimes the rational activitiy of the mind will continue below the subliminal level; it will go on far below the threshold of consciousness, in sleep and dream very often. It will yield ready forms of rational thought. Coleridge composed an originally long poem in dream. The problem of proper needle for the sewing machine was symbolically solved for its inventor in dream. Shelley poured out ready forms of poetry. Mathematical geniuses give ready calculation. But none of these are intuitional in the sense of the spiritual science. These activities do not permit conscious willing, except in a negligible measure. Also, they do not permit encroachment by reason. But, intuition, as developed by the disciplines of the spiritual science, widens the scope of reason, and makes conscious willing possible in the highest degree in every direction.

The Best Aspirations of Western Philosophy Are Fulfilled by the Intuition which Leads the Soul of Man to the Goal of Life, Consisting in the Realization of the Real

The important point to remember is that the solutions for the problems of religion, philosophy and science, lie in the development of intuition as shown by the ancient Sages. The goal of life which these Sages indicate, is Truth itself; the goal has been discerned in the clear perspective of complete knowledge, immediate and direct. The aim of life is the intuitive realization of the Self; for, the Self is the substratum for everything, the cause for everything, and the soul for everything. Western philosophers give no definite answers to such fundamental questions as, *"What is the goal of life?"* and *"What is the summum bonum?" "What is the supreme purpose of human life on earth?"* Whatever answers they provide, are in terms of the physical sciences, whose conclusions are formulated by the limitations of human mind, and on a non-metaphysical basis. By developing intuition, the spiritual East fulfils the best aspirations of the Western philosophy. Without the philosophy of intuition as it is practised in the East, the philosophy of the Western world reminds us of the helpless state of the physical science before the invention of the telescope, the microscope and the other special instruments of modern science. Before the invention of the microscope, it was not possible to know what the microbes were. Any attempt at a conjecture of the microscopic cells of life, or matter, must, obviously, have been a perfect failure.

To philosophize before developing all the higher and latent powers of observation that are there in man, cannot be really scientific, in so far as such a philosophy is infested with the errors and limitations of imperfect and undeveloped powers of perception and experience. Such a philosophizing will never succeed in engaging the attention of serious men of action, and can never yield any tangible results that could take up the life of mankind, in a powerful impact of upward movement. The proverb of the philosopher running after a black cat in a dark room, while the cat is not therein, must continue to hold its own, unless intuition is brought to action in the lives of the philosophers.

Intuition is the main method of the science of the Soul. Being essentially scientific, the spiritual science is capable of uniform application, and guarantees uniform results to the average man who trains himself in the methods laid down for the development of intuition.

The Nature of Intuition

Intuitional experience is a settled manifestation of the essential Light, and the intrinsic dynamism, of the inner self-existent Witness-Consciousness, in which the ultimate ground of all existence stands self-revealed. It determines the constant play of a plenary spiritual cognizance of the Consciousness of all existences, with the directness that belongs to a knowledge by total identity, and in the immediacy that goes with the inalienability of the oneness of one's own being with the Being of all beings.

A strong spiritual disposition long accustomed to an intimate self-observation in self-awareness, to a repeated reflection upon the self-existent truths of all things, the intrinsic *"why"*, *"how"*, *"where"*, *"what"*, *"when"* of all existences and all phenomena, acquires a mystical penetration into the Soul of all that is, and gains a light by which we grow into the Infinite.

It obtains the real Self-knowledge, accepts a temporary preoccupation with the realities of cosmic life, views the world by the world-transcending Consciousness, sees time and space by overstepping them, looks at life from a height pinnacled in the bosom of the awareness of the Absolute Awareness.

It lives permanently in a state of soul, a plenary vision, in which the direct and immediate experience of the transcendent Divinity is a natural condition, a constant self-sustaining status of being.

This, then is the intuitional experience to which the high spiritual intelligence of an austere dignity, uplifted beyond the constitutional fallibilities of the rational processes, the incertitudes of the intellectual findings, the instrumental futility of a metaphysically presupposed epistemology, – is a shining witness.

Again, of this intuitional experience, the high spiritual mind of integral insight that proceeds by the perception of the One in the many, and the many in the One, knows by the knowledge of an identity with the object of knowing, sees with the plenitude of Self-awareness and the all-aware Consciousness, is a grand observer and an invincible advocate.

Sensations and the Joy of Understanding

The animal part in man seeks sensations and the pleasures that arise from the disturbed, troubled and excited nerves. The higher part in man seeks the calm and peaceful light and joy of understanding.

When sensations dominate, the animal part grows stronger, dominant, renders the will weak, and demands the repetition of the sense-pleasures. When understanding dominates, the divine Consciousness emerges into action, and makes of will a power, of personality a greatness, of mind a haven of peace, and of life a heaven.

How to Reach Higher and Higher Forms of Inner Perception?

Close your eyes: You see nothing, the world of visible objects and persons is withdrawn from you. Close your ears: The world of hearing is lost to you. With the eyes, you cannot hear; and with the ears, you cannot see. Thus, the senses are limited in their capacity and functions. Each of our senses reveals only a fragment of the world.

See the world by the mind: You have quite broad and greater pictures. Perceive the world by poetic sensibility or aesthetic feeling, you have a different experience and perception. See the world by the clairvoyant vision, the invisible things become visible. See the world through the intuitive faculty and higher powers of the inner consciousness, you will find everywhere a divine Principle and Being.

The range of our perception is extended with every higher instrument of knowledge we employ. Man transcends the animal kingdom by reason of his richly endowed mental perception, and the Sage is lifted as much above the ordinary human individual by reason of his intuitive perception and experience of the wonders and delights of the creative Consciousness of the infinite Godhead.

The Dynamic Divine Knowledge

Divine dynamic Gnosis, or Vedānta, is a complexus of extraordinary cognitive disciplines of the contemplative Consciousness which rend veil after veil in the self-luminous self-perception, and lead the inner being to the Light beyond all lights.

Conditioned to the disciplines in the awareness of Awareness, of observing the Observer, witnessing the witnessing Self, the Vedāntic intelligence is a purified radiance raised above reason, proceeding by a method deeper and higher than the introspective evidence, substituting the intellectual assurances by experiential convictions, turning the feeling of the Infinite into the experience of the Infinite. It is a perpetual gymnastic in the gnostic powers of Self-perception, Self-vision, Self-experience, that transfigure the entire field of the individual life into an expanding arena, the receding horizons, of the one austere Self-seeing, seeing the Self in the Self, by the Self, the Self in all, and all in the Self, and seeking its delight in a knowledge structured above knowledge, Vedānta, Parāvidyā, in a Light beyond all lights, Jyotiṣām Jyotiḥ , in the Truth that transcends all truths, Satyasya Satyam.

Starting with the initial procedures of continually storing the chastened mind with profound philosophical perceptions which carry the power of stimulating into activity the native intuitions of the inner Being, the sustained reflection upon the fundamental truths concerning the Nature and the Being of the Transcendent, the unbroken energization of inner consciousness in a rapt contemplation, the formation of the psychosis of the Infinite*, – the Vedāntic consciousness submits itself in the immediacy of highest spiritual experience, to the Touches of the Transcendent.

Under their impact, it breaks the Infinite-psychosis, and finds its emergence into the Beyond that is the Beyond concerning which there can be no written work, much less an oral utterance, except a not easily comprehensible manual gesture, and from which there is no concession of a return.

---

* Psychosis of the Infinite = "Brahmākāra-Vṛtti" (ब्रह्माकारवृत्ति)

How the Soul is Organically Related to God

The identification of the inner intelligence with the Intelligence of the Divine is organic. If you take a glass of water and just drop it all in the ocean, the water becomes organically one with the rest of the ocean. If you take a piece of wood and throw it into the ocean, it does not become one with the ocean, it floats on the surface of the ocean, whereas the water has become one with the ocean. That is called organic identity and oneness with the ocean. Such an organic identity is established in inner spiritual conditions of illumination. The intelligence becomes one with the divine Intelligence. When it becomes one with the divine Intelligence, it becomes omnipresent, present at the same time in all places, even as the one ocean in the world which is artificially divided into five different oceans, is one, and this ocean is everywhere, here, there in Asia, there in Europe, there in Australia, in Africa, in South America, there at the North Pole, at the South Pole. At the same time it is everywhere, in the same moment it is everywhere.

The human intelligence which has found its organic identity with the divine Intelligence experiences Omnipresence, also Omnipotence, also boundless Knowledge, boundless Beauty, in a dimension other than our spatial dimension, – yet it penetrates our spatial dimension, includes our spatial dimension as a small speck of dust in its vast immeasurable Being.

We have to push forward and onward
the brilliance of our inquiring intelligence
and the luminous power of our questioning reason,
until the universe we live in and seek to study,
discloses to us its secrets, its laws,
the operative Consciousness behind it,
until Matter reveals to us the real substance
of which it is constituted,
until the supreme and invisible Divinity
becomes visible to us
through the veils of all manifestation,
until the all-merciful God
of infinite Consciousness and Perfection
is held in the arms of our inner experience,
until our intelligence itself becomes omniscient,
our personal will is completely dissolved
in the Will of the Divine
and our life is rendered into a vessel
that holds the splendours of the Divine.

Swami Omkarananda

Principles for a Life in the Divine

The true Lover of the Divine has several principles by which he lives – a life of principles. It is a life of principles, a life in the Divine. Among the many principles, some of the leading principles are:

The **Principle of Now**, that is to say, everything he does it **now**.

If you want to express great devotion for the Divine, please express it **now**, as much as is possible, to the maximum capacity possible. With a little stress and strain, fullest devotion express! If you want to pray intensively, please do it **now**!

Many people make many good resolves, spiritual resolves, but they postpone always: *"When I become old, I will be a Sannyasi."*

That way it does not help you. When you become old, your body becomes weak, prey to many diseases, and if there are no diseases, prey to weaknesses; if there are no weaknesses, prey to habits, old habits, which are difficult to get rid of, and without getting rid of those habits, you can't make spiritual progress. And apart from that, many attachments, with advancing age many attachments come in – Enkelkinder* – attachment to Enkelkinder, attachment to possessions, and so on. All kinds of things come

---

* Enkelkinder = grandchildren

out. And it becomes impossible for this old man to live a real spiritual life.

So, the spiritual individual does not postpone anything good, anything valuable, anything important, for the future. There is no tomorrow with him. Always it is **now**.

If you want to make the best speech in your life, make it **now**! Thereafter what happens, all your life you will be making the very best speeches.

Always do it now!

If you want to be charitable, do it **now**!

If you want to be good, be good **now**, not tomorrow!

If you want to be spiritual, be spiritual **now**!

If you want to build two houses, build them **now**, not tomorrow!

If you want to make a spiritual institution, make it **now**, not tomorrow!

If you want to write a book, try to write it **now**, not tomorrow! And so on.

Whatever it is, all good things, which you plan to do, do them **now** or be at them right now, so that at due time the right circumstances offer themselves and your aims will be fulfilled.

But the principle of **now** must always govern you with regard to everything that is **good**.

If anything doubtful is there, postpone it endlessly!

Only that which is noble, divine, good, generous, wonderful, moral, spiritual, has to be done instantly and now.

That is one of the principles that governs the life of the spiritual individual.

Another principle that governs his life is **Theocentricity**.

The principle of Theocentricity is: always **God-centered** – "Theo" is God – God-centered life, always God-centered, **everything for God**.

If he wants to make the best speech, it is **for God**.

If he wants to build a house, it is **for God**.

Everything in the name of God, for God, in order that one may come closer to the experience of God.

If he wants to keep best health now, he does it **now** and it is **for the sake of God**, not in order that the energies may be dissipated in sensual pleasures, but that the energies are directed towards the spiritual goals and which means that the whole inner nature stands transformed, all energies are turned towards the Divine, and uplifted, transformed, sublimated and made luminous and instruments of the Divine Light, and so forth.

So, always it is a God-centered life. **Everything for God**!

If he drives the car, it is **for God** and **with God, through God** and so forth.

Every purpose is subordinated to the central purpose of God-experience and God-thought, God-feeling.

God stands always first and therefore it is a God-centric life.

The principle of **Theocentricity** is one of the many principles that governs the true aspirant on the path.

The Supreme Creative Principle

How the Worlds Came into Existence

The two Dimensions of the Divine are the Manifest and the Unmanifest. The manifested Universe has come from some Power of the unmanifested Reality. This supreme transcendental Reality is motionless, immutable, all-perfect. This we have called the unmanifested Reality, but, in fact, this unmanifested Reality is there everywhere in the Manifestation. Within the Unmanifest one Portion has come forth – the manifested Reality, and some Intelligence of the Divine, called God, the Creator, is maintaining This.

Within us and all around us there is the blazing Reality of the all-seeing God. We are brought into existence by the Love of God; we are being sustained by the Delight of God. The entire Cosmos, all Manifestation, all Matter, all Space is filled with the infinite Delight of the divine Consciousness.

At every Point, in every Atom, there is the Centre of this infinite Happiness of the infinite Consciousness. Not only our inner spiritual Being, but every Nerve and Bone, every Cell is a Point of the infinite Delight of the infinite Consciousness. Therefore, everything in creation longs for Happiness, searches for Happiness. Happiness is the Aim of everybody's activity; Happiness is the Goal of all life.

The whole creation is moving towards happiness. Why does it search for happiness? Why does it long for happiness? We search only for that which we have lost, not for something which we possess. Our nature, which is the infinite Happiness of the infinite Consciousness, is lost to our experience and understanding, and therefore we are looking for happiness, searching for happiness.

Man in general is restlessly conquering the outer world. Though man steps on and walks on the moon, man is not a grain happier for it, nor has he solved even one millionth of his problems. He is more miserable for his conquest of the moon; he has new fears, he has new problems to face.

No matter how much wealth you have, how many houses and buildings you own in many countries of the world, or how much beauty, how much physical strength you have, no matter how fine your senses be and what keen pleasures they bring you – you are restless and unhappy. Something in your heart creates disturbance, a sense of want. You will always look for something else. You are condemned to do so, as long as you are in creation. No matter who you are, whether a poet, a rich man, a king, a genius, no matter what you are, you will be perpetually restless. The Spirit in you would have no satisfaction worth mentioning. You will be always seeking, even if you do not know what you are seeking. So, all empirical search for happiness is an attempt, an outward attempt, to regain the happiness that we have lost.

In Reality, in Truth, there is nothing anywhere except God as infinite creative Consciousness, as Beauty and infinite Happiness. Matter, mind, life are manifestations derived from the Consciousness. The human individual, not knowing this Truth, ignorant of this fact, driven by a sense of multiplicity, finds only the many in the experience. He does not see God. He sees many things in the world, he has the experience of the many, and therefore he is constantly exposed to suffering, for he is in the untruth. What is the Truth? The Truth is everywhere GOD ALONE. The world is in Him, He is in it, He is the world, He is more than the world. All is resident in Him. He is the first and the last Truth.

All creation has emerged from the Fire of Thought of the Divine, the Fire of creative Intelligence in the Divine. Thought is present everywhere, even as the dream in the mind of an individual is a product of thought, even as all the works of the human individual – whether they are buildings or books, or any other things – are a product of thought. The infinite Mind, the infinite Intelligence, is present everywhere, vibrant in all metals, vibrant and active in the mind of man, in all living forms, vibrant and active everywhere, in every point of space. The whole matter is vibrant with the Consciousness and Intelligence of God!

Numberless universes have risen and disappeared. Let us say, every universe lasts for several millions of years. After that what happens? Perhaps there is another creation.

From the timeless bosom of the infinite Reality another universe comes into manifestation. Like thoughts rising and disappearing, like dreams rising and disappearing, numberless thoughts and dreams rise and disappear in the infinite Intelligence of the Divine. From where have they come? And where have they gone? Who bears them? It is the timeless Reality. That Being which is timeless bears in Itself all time-eternities. Our universe is one among the countless universes that have risen and disappeared, and there will be countless numbers of universes in the future. Who is great, this beautiful universe or That Which has founded the universe, That from Which this universe has come as a temporary structure which will soon disappear, even if that 'soon' be millions and millions of years? Certainly the Creator is the greater.

Let us suppose you are dreaming. In the dream state you create a magnificent universe, with stars, planets, and so on. You are supervising what you have created. Suddenly, somebody comes and wakens you. The moment you open your eyes, all the universe has dissolved. Where has it gone? Back into your consciousness. Yet you can create it again. So, when God wants it, He can instantaneously re-manifest. That infinite Consciousness created billions and billions of cosmic cycles. When we look at the sky, we see the planets, we see the stars. Each of these stars is a universe in itself. It is an unimaginable boundless creation. It is childish to say that the universe is created for the first time. What was there before this universe came into existence? Perhaps another universe. What was there before that? Perhaps some other manifestation. What was there before that? You can go on questioning, and you will find endless numbers of universes that have risen and disappeared.

Not all the creation is important – all these worlds are mere expressions of the Divine. These expressions are not important. The Creator of all these expressions is all-important! Expressions come and go; the creative Spirit behind is eternal and perpetual. The whole universe is like a fleeting dream in the Mind of God. Such dreams He had by the millions, and such dreams He will have endlessly. Such dreams come and go. What is all-important is the Divine Itself, the supreme creative Spirit.

Man in the Creation

Man is an externalization of Consciousness. The divine Intelligence in the human individual, with the help of which we perceive colours and everything, with the help of which the intelligence of man is functioning, this divine Reality in the human individual which is the source of all our experience – this is the same as the supreme divine Reality! That is to say: this Reality of the Divine in the human individual which is sustaining all experiences – be it a perception of colour, or hearing a sound, or responding to human love – this Being which makes all these experiences possible – that is the same as the divine

Reality, the absolute Existence.

The human individual is a structure of the infinite superconscious Being, caught up in the network of self-ignorance. Man is an ontological being, not a physical being. He is a natural being seen empirically, seen psychologically and materially. But this natural being is only an outer structure in which the ontological, the superconscious Being is resident and indwelling. Man is primarily a creative Spirit, for he is made in the Image of the Divine. God's very Nature is supreme Creativity. He is the supreme Genius, He is the Source of all genius. In every man is the highest creative Principle. From that Principle, with this Principle the supreme Divinity has fashioned all the universes and filled all these universes with all kinds of wealth and values.

The highest Principle is unfortunately imperceptible to the human physical eye, and unfortunately also imperceptible to the perceiving intelligence in man. Yet that ultimate Principle can be experienced by the very faculty by which a great scientist discovers new things; with that very faculty by which the poet creates new words and new images and awakens new emotions; by that very faculty with which a businessman becomes more efficient; by that very faculty by which a thinker becomes a genius; by that very capacity by which a great writer becomes the greatest writer, a great inventor the greatest inventor. What is that faculty? It is the meditating capacity, the contemplating capacity. Even God Himself brings all the universe into existence by contemplation.

How does the poet create? How does the sculptor shape new forms? How does the scientist discover something new? How does the engineer construct something extraordinary and unique in the history of engineering? By contemplation, by deep thought. How does Homer or a great epic writer bring the whole story into existence? Through contemplation. By contemplation God makes manifest the whole creation, even as the poet or a great creator, a creative artist in any field, brings magnificent phenomena into being. The capacity to obtain and present greatest thoughts is a gift of the Intelligence of the Spirit. A capacity of poetic expression, a capacity for a creative life are expressions or gifts of the Spirit within. This marvellous Presence of the Divine is in everyone, and it is a great blessing to grow ever more conscious of this fact.

There is a unique building, extraordinary for its structure, extraordinary even in its details, extremely complex. How did this wonderful building come into existence? It is the projection of the architect, the designer. God projects this universe through contemplation.

Through contemplation the aim is attained; through contemplation new things are discovered; through contemplation something is brought into being, something is obtained. It is a capacity that has to be developed. It can be developed; everybody can be contemplative. In fact, everyone is contemplative. Meditation is as pervasive as life; wherever there is life, even in a unicellular organism, there is concentration, meditation, contemplation. It is a natural capacity with which you are born. By this very capacity you can experience God, you can know the Truth. There is no other way of knowing the Truth.

An all-creative Spirit is present everywhere. It is in the crystals, in the sea, in the sand, in the wind, in all forms of life. Look at Nature; it constantly changes itself, forms itself, expresses itself, presents new beauties, survives destruction and puts forth newer and newer forms of expression. It is the creative Intelligence of the Divine that is ensouling all Nature. It is the creative Intelligence of the Divine that is always present within you, constantly ready to serve you, to help you conquer situations and make progress. All is created by God in Himself, with His own Image of Peace, Happiness, Perfection, Beauty, Harmony, Order, Fullness. To see anything other than God is to be punished, is to be human, is to be conditioned, is to be ignorant. Man in the world does not experience God; therefore, he is exposed to suffering, is limited in knowledge, knows death, experiences diseases, makes a tremendous waste of life's resources. For this reason the knowledge of the Divine is of supreme importance. It changes our life, It dwells in our intelligence and guides it to higher and higher stages of evolution. It is the secret of true happiness.

Life in the physical body is temporary; everything

that it seeks after is also temporary. Anything temporary, no matter how pleasant it can be, no matter what it promises, is something that is going to fail us. Even if you have everything that the creation can offer you, you will still be wanting; though there is nothing missing, there still is discontentment in you, still there is some frustration, some fundamental and residual restlessness. Therefore, wisdom compels the seeking and earnest heart to shift its central interest on the Creator.

There is infinite celestial Music within you! And that is why you are restlessly seeking for delights of music. And even if you were Bach, you would struggle and strive after greater melodies. That which is in you is infinite Harmony, infinite Melody, and you shall not find satisfaction until you have discovered that which is in you. All the wonderful music produced in the world is the enjoyment of the endless Music within. Where is the end of the striving after musical perfection in a great musician? Only in the endless Music, in the infinite Music. Till then musicians will always be born in the world – each greater than the preceding one – yet they will be striving after greater and greater perfection in the field of music. In this tendency each reveals that there is infinite Harmony and Melody and Music within himself.

There is endless Light within man; and in his tendency to seek after light, the light of knowledge, in his search for wisdom, in his search for perfection, he reveals what is within him. Even a carpenter wants to be perfect, the ironsmith wants to be perfect, the cobbler wants to be perfect, everybody wants to be perfect – be it in the field of work, in the field of their knowledge, in the field of their skills, or in the field of the entire life. Perfection is what every man aims at and thus reveals what is hidden within himself: infinite Perfection.

There is endless knowledge within you. All your outer striving for knowledge, for ever more knowledge, is an apologetic attempt to arrive at the endless Knowledge within you. There is endless Peace within you; and therefore you shall never be satisfied – however much peace may be given – until you discover and experience the endless Peace within you which is God, which is the Truth.

All human problems can ultimately be reduced to the simple fact that there is deep in your soul something great which is satisfied by nothing, which could be satisfied only by infinite Joy, infinite Love, infinite Life, infinite Knowledge, infinite Beauty and Power which are characteristic and natural attributes of the divine Spirit within you. This greatest Being is your real Life of life. That has to be befriended. The greater your contact with the Divine, the more blessed you are, the more wonderful you are, the more peaceful you are. Eternal life is given to you in consequence of your close relations to the Divine.

All science is purely aiming at the conquest of creation. On account of that it is absolutely unable to grant man peace or wisdom worth the name. All science, therefore, fails us. Nothing in creation can satisfy us, can solve the fundamental problems of life, the riddles of life, can grant us Immortality, everlasting Peace, creative Intelligence, everlasting Joy. No matter what the sciences gain for us, it is something within creation; and nothing in creation is of any value where the fundamental questions of life and soul are concerned. Science says: "*We will create new energy.*" But in creating new energy also new problems will be created. We are not happy for the petrol we have, though it brings us much comfort. And when petrol comes to an end, you are miserable. You produce another energy, and you will produce it from some other resources in creation. Again that comes to an end, creating new problems. Nothing in creation can satisfy the heart of man. So, all sciences from this standpoint are useless, are more a disservice than a service; but any science that turns its attention to the Creator is a great science, an immortal science, leading to the conscious experience of the Immortal, leading us to sources and resources which are inexhaustible. Biology pertains to creation, physics pertains to creation, economics, all social sciences, all material sciences pertain to creation. These will not help us ultimately. Seek for that knowledge which is not pertaining to creation but pertaining to the Creator.

Science has enabled man to step on the moon but has completely destroyed the environment; it has destroyed the earth, its natural resources, its pure air, everything it has destroyed. That which seems to be a blessing turns out to be a curse. There are problems above problems. Nothing in creation has the real solution to the problems of life. The solution to the problems of life lies in only one place: in the Hands of the Creator.

The doctor is within the creation, and he has not the solution to the problems of life. He is himself worried; his ability to help is limited. The rich man has not the solution to the problems of life. The most beautiful person, or the most gifted person, the most desired person has no solution to the serious problems of life. Nothing in creation, not all its beauty, not all its wealth nor all its resources can make you a little happier. If they make you a little happy, quickly that happiness is overcome by other problems. Even if you embrace the whole creation as your personal possession, you shall never be happy.

Perhaps the birds all over the world join together to make perpetual music for you; all the beautiful rivers and the seas of the world may wash your feet in honour of you – even then you will not be happy. Perhaps all the factories around the world will be busy producing whatever you want – even then you will not be happy. Perhaps all people, all mankind become poets and begin to write praises of you – even then your heart will find no rest and peace. While your face smiles at the praises that man can give you, secretly the heart within is being torn by its own sorrow.

The problems of life resolve themselves the moment we learn to dwell consciously in the Creator. From one point of view we are already living in the Creator, but we are not conscious of it. If all could grow conscious of this fact that we live, move and have our being in the Creator, then everyone would lose the limitations of being a creature. Everyone would then subsist in unbreakable peace and joy, wisdom and freedom. Consciously to live, move and have our being in the Creator, in oneness with the One, is the key and the solution to the riddle of human life.

How to experience everything as one? How to live in an ecstatic, all-absorbing God-Consciousness? We must be in a position to think like God, feel like God, live like God, before we can realize and express His infinite Perfection, Peace, Beauty, Light. How does God think, how does God feel, how does God work? Human feeling is limited, narrow, conditioned, relative, troubled. God's feeling is unlimited, all-perfect, untroubled. Human love is limited, mixed up with dislike and hatred, governed by conditions, time and space. God's Love is unlimited. Therefore, you must constantly seek to express unlimitedness. It is true, physical conditions make it impossible for us to serve every son of the earth, and we are only able to serve our own children; but we should include all other children at least in our thoughts and prayers and feelings. When we are walking in the street, let us say in our hearts: *"May all humanity be peaceful, may all be blessed; may there be peace and happiness and joy and progress everywhere on earth."*

Let our life be a continued festival of pouring blessings, peace, happiness, joy, strength upon the world. Let us also bless and have the greatest goodwill and love for creatures and beings which are invisible, and also for beings who are in other worlds. Let us breathe a blessing and a thought of peace and love even for children who are not yet born and who will be born a thousand years later on earth.

The Universe as a Projection of the Divine

All manifestation is a projection of God Himself!
He is maintaining this entire creation. He closes His Eyes, He dissolves the creation, and He can re-create it, re-manifest it instantly if He likes. And nobody is really destroyed, because all is re-absorbed into the divine Existence, into the Consciousness Divine. This is the scheme of creation.

It is God appearing as the universe!
Do not be deceived by the appearances but experience the Substance. And the Substance is of the nature of infinite Light, infinite Peace, Joy, Power, Grace, Beauty which is appearing as the world, as the people around, as the sounds, as the colours. All this external life is a manifestation of the Divine and, therefore, divine. This, if perverted, one mistakes for the whole of the Reality,

the whole of the Divinity, and one plunges into this by forgetting the original fact that there is something above this and beyond this. And what is this external life? Only a partial expression of the Divine. Momentarily, for the human mind there is appearing something called 'the world'. In Truth, there is no such thing as the world – there is only a nameless, formless, all-wonderful divine Consciousness. We assume the world to be an expression of the Divine. And through the world the Divine has to be experienced. And when the Divine is experienced, one has to express into this world something of the treasures of the Divine. This is the philosophy of our institution.

All creatures are God manifest, edged into limitation. And these limitations are further worsened by a personality, constructed as a result of these limitations, which are the psychic being, the unconsciousness and the outer mind. The physical body of man, man's organism, is such that it permits this God to present Himself in man, to see Himself, experience Himself and know Himself. For this reason he is superior to all creatures. It is, therefore, a very rare gift to have a physical human body; it is the first great gift of God. Through the body man can achieve the Perfection of the omnipresent God. Remember the Truth: everywhere there is space only for God! The world is created by God and is a field of experience of God; it is a stage on which we can attain unending Peace, Happiness, Power, Knowledge, Wisdom, Beauty.

There are several invisible worlds interpenetrating this

visible universe. The subtlest of all worlds is the Divine Itself. It is penetrating everything, is sustaining everything by being the inner Essence in everything. And this Essence in everything is so subtle, so supra-electronic, so sensitive, so rich in capacities, that being in everything It feeds everything, sustains everything and develops highest capacities. If you know this, you will always have a background feeling that all matter is vibrant with the Presence of the Divine. It takes a scientist to discover that all is formed of energy. And it takes a Truth-seer, a God-knower, to discover that all is the bearer of the Divine.

Man, in a state of highest purity and when touched by the Grace of God, experiences the outer world as God, as Reality, as a structure of the divine Being. The difference in experiencing the world – whether materially or spiritually – lies in the inner vision. When our inner vision is divine, exalted, spiritual, then we see another world, a wonderful divine Presence everywhere in the world.

To be touched by the Grace of God is the same as to possess the Wisdom of God.

You are constantly filled with a strange inner joy, a continual inner peace, inner light and love. You are perpetually creative, even though you may not do anything. Your Spirit is active, is expressive. Blessings flow from your heart to the whole creation. You perceive the Divine everywhere. The Presence of the Divine is constantly felt in all living things, it is felt in the whole sky, all around you. The Presence of the Divine is incessantly acknowledged by you, within and without. You live in the Face of the Divine, under the Eyes of the Divine. It is then that you become a perpetual blessing to all creation. No matter that you do not talk to anyone, or may not even be serving anyone, it is yet completely true that you are a great blessing to every creature; you are a perpetual blessing to the whole creation. Then you are filled with Light of the divine Presence, you are full of the Wisdom of God, you are full of the creative Knowledge of God.

You then lead a beautiful and blessed life which is not only beautiful and blessed for yourself but for thousands – for the very air around you, for the whole space around you, for all invisible creatures around you, for all visible things around you... You can contribute to reaching this goal by being always in a spiritual state of consciousness. Be always aware that God is surrounding you; that you are never separated from Him; that He is all-seeing, all-merciful and all-blessing; that you are in Him, and He is in you; that your only duty is to express wisdom, express love, express goodness, express good actions. Develop your aspirations and your faith. Always bless the world; always be in a positive state, in a state made up of faith; feel the all-seeing Divinity within and around you. And if you continue your spiritual practices, your capacities are endless and unlimited.

The whole cosmos is tied to every individual in the universe.

If somebody hits you on the toe, you feel it at once; and if somebody touches your head, at once you feel it, because the whole body is an organic whole. Nobody can touch any stone, or dry leaf, or any being or person in the world without the whole cosmos feeling it. It is not poetry but a fact that, when a good man or devotee of the Divine is walking by, secretly the whole Nature, material and immaterial, animate and inanimate, delights. The whole Nature is indebted to him, because he releases into Nature most harmonious, unifying, integrating, uplifting influences. In mythology you find people saying: *"Oh, tree, be my witness!"* Sometimes, in mythology you find that even matter, the earth, is made to be witness. It is not poetry but a scientific fact that there is an all-seeing Intelligence even in inanimate matter and of which matter does not know; likewise as in man there is the all-knowing divine Reality of which man himself knows nothing.

Even in minerals the infinite divine Presence is existent.

It is present with all Its Perfection, with all Its Omniscience, Its Omnipotence and Omnipresence. It is behind there as the central Witness and as the rudimentary Soul. This Soul in the mineral grows, develops and becomes a feeling in the plant; therein is the animal's lust and greed, hatred and jealousy. In man there are all these, plus will-power, plus many faculties and capabilities. The human kingdom is the crown of creation and, therefore, the supreme value and importance of human life.

How to define each stage of evolution: mineral, plant,

animal, man? What is the difference from one step to another? The difference is of material nature. Alongside the material differences, there is the difference in life form. Alongside the life form differences, there are structural, organic and mental differences as well as differences in consciousness. Man's brain organism is so developed that it makes other faculties, which are absent in the lower animals, come into operation. In that way the fullest expression of the latent consciousness, the latent life in many-sided expression is made possible to the extent where every innovation, improvisation, insight, imagination in man can be implemented and his experience enriched, thus enriching everything. So, it is a difference in the structure through which the latent consciousness and life express themselves. In the man stage the structure and basis permitting life and consciousness to come into expression are so far developed that here man is supreme in creation.

All is Consciousness

We do not live in a material universe but in a spiritual universe.

All matter can be converted into energy; all energy can be converted into Consciousness. Two forms of this Consciousness are matter and mind. Matter is a manifestation of Consciousness, in Consciousness, as Consciousness. And there is on the other hand the mind.

This, too, is Consciousness. So, everywhere there is Consciousness. By Consciousness we mean that which transcends even this empirical awareness. It is absolute Consciousness. God is absolute Intelligence, absolute Awareness, absolute Consciousness. The human awareness is limited; there are conditions in which it flows.

The supreme divine Consciousness is present everywhere in all its infinite Perfection.

There is in you a Divinity which is supremely perfect. All your spiritual progress pertains only to your outer individual being and to your soul; it has no relation to the Infinite. That is already there in the individual in you, unaffected by the individual and its limitations and bondages. It is the soul that evolves until it realizes its background: the infinite all-perfect Being. Then it becomes one with the Divine, at the human stage and beyond the human stage. Evolution is only possible for that which is limited; that which is unlimited cannot evolve, it is already fully evolved, perfect.

Merged into the Divine, having become one with the One, the soul is completely absorbed in the Consciousness of the One. This Consciousness is omnipresent, omnipotent, omniscient. Aware of the Omnipotence of God within him, above him, around him, there is no reason for man to fear anything, to feel weak at any time; it is impossible for him to think anything wrong, feel anything wrong, make any mistakes. His mind is made to understand, experience and express this Omnipotence of the Divinity within him. When we are absorbed in the Consciousness of the One, where is anything that can confront us, limit us, distress us…

The million varieties of things that you see in the world are formed by one Being: GOD – with His own Substance, in His own Substance, in Himself, of Himself. If you do not see Him there, you are in the field of untruth, you are materialistic, you are sensuous, you are limited, you are cut off from infinite Happiness, Peace, Power, Beauty. When you do not live in God, you are in the field of untruth, you are in a world which is deprived of true light; you then are a source of unhappiness to yourself and to others, though your works are admired by human beings. Therefore, do your best in order to be in tune with the world of God. See everywhere what there is: the Presence of the Divine.

There is nothing wrong in planting beautiful rose plants; but if you do not see God in them and also in the hands that are planting and also in the earth and all around – you are in the field of untruth. You are exposing yourself to difficulties, and there is much danger for you.

Since the whole universe is also of psychic substance, it can be transformed by the psychical principle in man. Everything can appear to him as he wants it. If he wants everything to be peaceful, he can experience it to be peaceful. If he wants to experience everything as the Divine, he can experience everything as the Divine. But if his mental state is too low and primitive – though the highest Reality is present everywhere behind the psychical veil of the universe – he will experience only unhappiness, misery, problems, difficulties, trials. Even as the mountain and the iron poles in the dream are nothing but made of psychical structure and not actually material, though they seem to be material – even so all the universe external is made of psychical structure, not material, though it seems to be material.

The following story may illustrate the above said: In a corner of the studio of a great artist there was a wonderful black stone. All the inmates of the house of the sculptor have been always referring to it as *'the stone'*. One day the sculptor has carved of it a beautiful image of a woman. From that day the sculptor and the inmates of that house have been always calling it *'the woman'*. They have been always observing it, looking at it as a woman, even talking of it as *'the woman'*. The idea that it is *'the woman'* has gone deeply into their unconscious mind. There was no trace of any thought that it was and is only a stone. All that had happened to the stone was that a little of its shape has been disturbed. The stone as such had disappeared for them, and to them it is *'the woman'*. In truth it is the same stone, it is nothing but a stone.

Even so the human mind takes the appearances as world, refers to it as *'the world'*, suffers by it or perceives pleasures in it, while the Truth is: it is nothing but God Himself! God alone is all that is, within, around, everywhere. All this is God Himself, as the woman, as the stone. Even as the woman is nothing but the stone itself in another shape, so is the world God Himself in another shape. The human mind has mistaken God for the world, as the sculptor and the others in that house have mistaken the stone for the woman. All problems begin to arise the moment you forget that **the world is nothing but God Himself.**

The Divinity in Man

Man is not merely a creature among many creatures in creation but the bearer of the Creator in creation, and therefore, by that very reason, supremely great.
He is greater than the creation. Without that Creator he is nothing more than a dry and broken reed. It is the Presence of the Creator in the inner Spirit of man that makes him greater than the creation. With that much of greatness that you bear in your soul, why have you to beg about for small solutions of the created universe?

Creature that you are, you are greater than creation!
Is that not a paradox, a puzzle? You are not even stronger than a pebble, yet you are greater than the creation! What makes this possible for you? The mere fact that the Creator dwells in your inner being. By this reason you are infinitely greater than the creation, no matter how great the creation is, how valuable everything within creation be...

Look at the great emperors of the world in the last

two thousand years. Each thought he would make himself happy by conquering new lands, by having much wealth, by having many pleasures. Almost every emperor had everything that he wanted, but few mortals were more miserable than those emperors, and few have met a death that they have met with.

This is the most wonderful thing about you: though you are yourself a product of the product that the universe is, you carry in yourself the Creator! This is the one factor which elevates you above the universe. As long as this is so, you are, theoretically at least, assured of total freedom from the limitations that the universe imposes on you. You can make this a practical fact by your personal striving. The Creator is infinitely greater than everything that is created; He is within you while all the time transcending you.

Let us say, in a bottle there is space or air. Though the air is inside the bottle, there is also air outside the bottle, it transcends the boundaries of the bottle. Even so the Spirit, called the Creator, while dwelling in your inner being, transcends the limitations of your body, of your mind, of every psychological principle in you. This fact makes you the crown of creation; it sets on you unending dignity and **makes you heir to everything the Divine has!**

Everything that is visible in the universe is nothing compared to that which is within you!

That is why a holy scripture in its wonderful wisdom says: *"That which is within you is greater than that which is without you!"*

What is without you? The whole universe, the sun and the moon and the stars, the planets, the entire cosmos – all this is outside you. But what is outside you – no matter if it be immeasurable space, or endless mountains of gold and diamonds, or endless seas of milk and butter and honey, no matter what it is, what power it is, what value it is – all this is smaller than what is within you. What is within you is always the greater. If you can conceive of something very great, be sure that there is something greater than that, and that is within you. What could be that marvellous thing? It is the Divine, God, the Creator! It is this fact that is the cause for your restlessness. You are conscious of something great, but you are not definite about what it is. You hunger for something great, but you do not know what it is.

The waters of the world can be exhausted – but nothing can exhaust the resources in the creative Intelligence of the Creator. All resources in the Creator are inexhaustible, unlimited. Use them unlimitedly, endlessly, still they are endless and unlimited. Inexhaustible resources – be it in water, in power or energy, be it in intelligence, in genius or life, be it in art or beauty, in peace, freedom, happiness, in all you can think of – are in the Creator.

Though God produces endless numbers of geniuses,

numberless universes, His Wisdom and His creative Capacities do not wane. He has endless possibilities. Countless numbers of universes like this may appear and disappear. Scientists say, many stars have already died, though they are still visible to us. Many universes have already disappeared, and many more are on the way to disappear. What is this mysterious intelligence from which all this emerges? God, a mighty Presence, present within every man, in all creation, while at the same time transcending creation. It is not caught up in the universe which It has projected. It is always infinitely greater than the universe.

Man, as he is constituted, seems to be a helpless, tiny creature in this gigantic world of gigantic powers and forces. Yet such a man has the highest redeeming Principle in him, the whole of the Creator is in him. The Image of God is not different from God Himself, it is one and the same; there are no two Gods. This Divinity holds the key to all our problems. It is the true and the final and consummate fulfilment of life.

Turn to the Creator, and you will find numberless inner resources serving you.

No matter what energy science can create in consequence of the best functioning of the best genius of the best scientist – it will have an end, it will be accompanied by problems. Yet no one can exhaust the love in your heart, no one can exhaust the peace in your heart, no one can exhaust the joy, the beauty, the knowledge in your being if you have contacted the Creator. The earlier you recognize this fact, the more noble, dignified, valuable your life becomes. All that you need to do every day is to turn a little of your thoughts towards the Divine, the Creator, and, when possible, devote a little time to Him, do some selfless service, seek to develop your love and extend it to creation. How valuable your life is, how wonderful you are, rests upon how profitably you use every hour of your life for the acquisition of this Wisdom of God. It is the knowledge of this boundless, all-witnessing, all-knowing, all-creative Intelligence that adds a new and boundless worth to your life. Without such a knowledge life is worthless, is deprived of its real dignity; therefore, knowledge of the Divine is the fundamental necessity.

Be an embodiment of the Wisdom of God!

Be full of the knowledge of God, walk as an embodiment of the knowledge of God – and you will have a thousand blessings. You will have perpetual peace, you will have endless resources. You are independent in your happiness and, therefore, can make others happy. Others can profit from you, depend upon your wisdom, derive strength from your wisdom, find new outlooks and inspiration in their lives through your wisdom. It even may be that through your aid they come closer to God and become themselves independent sources of strength and peace and joy for others.

You have a thousand ways out of creation open for you, ways out of the limitations which are characteristic of creation. Many great men of God have established in many conditions and circumstances and situations of life relations with the Creator. While washing the dishes, a Saint has established relations with the Creator. As a housewife you may become the greatest creature among the creatures in the universe by the kind of relations you establish with the Divine. Every little thought devoted to the Divine enriches you in a manner as nothing in creation can enrich you, even if you possess the whole of it. Therefore, wisdom tells us: turn to the Divine! You have twenty-four hours in a day. Devote at least twenty seconds or twenty minutes to the Divine, and you will be richer for it; you will be more peaceful for it; you will find new channels struck in order that the resources from the Creator may come into you – the creature within the creation. These channels will constantly feed you with inexhaustible resources. The creature within creation that man is owes himself the duty of somehow discovering the Creator and establishing relations with Him, of discovering the Divine and establishing relation with It.

Wherever you may be, in whatever circumstances you may be, just think of the Creator – and you will find the Creator thinking of you a thousand times! He has a million hearts, and He has one boundless Heart of infinite and inexhaustible Love. Every little thought concerning the Creator compels the Creator to think of you a thousand times. Thus you will be led from one reality to another, until you discover that which is the greatest of all greatest things: the Truth, the Timeless, the Infinite, the Eternal, the Divine, the Absolute! If you befriend that Divinity, you attain eternal life, you are liberated from the hold of the universe. Everything that is within the universe is subject to the conditions which have formed the universe, and these conditions tyrannize the human spirit. Man longs for peace, and peace is nowhere to be found.

There is only **one** way you can find rest and peace and joy and power and strength in life; catch the Creator! That is your Lover, that is your Father, that is the Soul of your life, that is the Secret of all satisfaction, that is the supreme creative Principle! Befriend the Creator, talk to Him, converse with Him, cultivate relations with Him. He is all-sensitive. Every word of yours is heard by Him; every thought of yours is seen by Him; every feeling in your heart is felt by Him. He responds to you in a way that nothing else in the world can respond to you. Before your own ears can hear your own words, He hears you. He is closer to your words than your tongue. He is the pervading Reality, the Intelligence of intelligence, the Space of space, the supreme creative Principle.

Try to establish in your own way relations with the Divine Being, with That which is the Greatest of the greatest, which knows everything everywhere, which is sustaining everything everywhere, and which is transcending everything everywhere. Maybe by meditation, or by prayer, or by the noblest conduct, or by devotion, or by any other method, or by all methods – try to establish relations with this supreme Creator. Merely to address the Creator is a great gain. Human history is full of examples of persons who have conversed with the infinite Peace, who have experienced the eternal Life while being in the mortal body, who have tasted boundless infinite Power while yet being helplessly caught up in this physical form. Though being in the limitations in which we are in this universe, we can still, here and now, experience That which transcends the universe while sustaining the universe.

The whole genius of life in creation lies in its capacity to experience the Creator.

Every creature is richer for a mere awareness of the Creator. The creature is destined to perish – whether it is a lizard or a fly, a bird or fish, whether it is an elephant, a lion, a snake, a man, no matter what the creature is – it has formed a body that perishes. Every creature is a perishable thing; the whole creation itself is perishable. Though the creation endures beyond our bodies, though the creation has a longer life than the creatures – everything is perishable. In this perishability the only way out is to have a hold on the Creator. To have a hold on the Creator is to lose our mortality, to lose the fear of death. The possibility of perishing is taken away the moment we have a hold on the Imperishable, on the Creator. Not only is the mortality lost and a conscious awareness of immortality gained, but one also dwells in a perpetual delight, in ever new joy, in the fullness of joy. Therein is the true satisfaction; therein is the real rest for man. Nothing in life is a greater goal or is more valuable. Blessed are those creatures who seek to befriend the Creator.

All that you see or hear or think of is within creation. The whole creation as such is marked by perishability, by imperfection; no matter what it is, it shares the characteristics of the creation which is imperfect. Therefore, it becomes the duty of everything created to turn towards the Creator, to befriend the Creator, to reflect upon the Nature of the Creator, to find roads and ways by which one can contact the Creator, to live in the Creator while yet living within the creation.

Always try to befriend the Creator!

When all friends in life fail you, this Friend will never fail you. When wealth fails you, this Wealth will never fail you; it is ever creative Wealth, it is inexhaustible Wealth. So, wisdom says, keep, if not both, at least one eye upon the Divine! That would be sufficient to establish for you every kind of security. It also would be sufficient to cause in you that wisdom which will awaken a third eye in you that is constantly focussed on the Divine. From such a focussing you will draw resources which are non-existent in the whole creation.

What do you need: something in creation or the Creator Himself?

To ask for and to strive after that which is in creation is asking for and striving after that which is perishable, something that falls away through your fingers. Every man in the world strives for something or the other within creation; and he is the greatest who strives after the Creator Himself. To strive after the Creator, to make the Creator dwell in our hearts, walk with us, be with us in all conditions – this is the greatest blessing, this is the ultimate fulfilment of life, this is to have something which nothing in creation can ever give. Everything in creation, no matter how precious and valuable it be, is infinitely less than the Creator.

Liberation ultimate and absolute is possible because you are not a condemned creature in creation but a creature bearing the whole of the Creator in yourself! This is the security and assurance of your total liberation and freedom. For true freedom, true peace, true joy of life, and for eternal life you have to turn to the Creator, the highest Principle within the creation, and the highest Principle transcending all that is created.

May the Divine open in your blessed lives many ways by which you are in constant contact with the supreme Creator. May your love and your wisdom secure for you many forms of relations with the Creator and make your life a thing eternal in the mortal field, in the field of creation. Even when the creation disappears, that which is eternal in you remains, has perpetual fulfillment in itself, ever new fulfilment, absolute fulfilment.

The Life in the Ashram

The life in the Ashram is a life in the Divine.

All works are divine works.

All thoughts are divine thoughts.

All feelings are divine feelings.

All life is made divine in nature.

Something of that which is in you,
the Eternal and the Infinite – Perfection –
is made manifest outwardly.

It is experienced. When it is experienced
man remains in the Divine and
the Divine remains in him.

If he eats, it is the Divine eating.

If he works, it is the Divine working.

If he speaks, it is the Divine speaking.

One lives in the other, the other lives in one.

God lives in this person and this person lives
in God.

This stage arrives. When this stage arrives,
your life is really blessed and divine.

So, try to see that all through the day you cultivate virtues, unfold spirituality, constantly watch thoughts and feelings and turn them into divine thoughts and feelings.

In this process the Mantra repetition is a powerful help, constant Mantra repetition, constant Mantra listening, constant company with godly personalities, people who inspire, elevate, uplift by their behaviour, by their talk, by their looks, by their whole gesture, and by their life style.

Company with such personalities is a great blessing.

Forms of Prayer

There is the prayer of the heart. There is a mental prayer. There is an oral prayer. There are many forms of prayers. Some prayers go by the name of meditation. The prayer of a man of knowledge consists in a constant and continuous awareness that God is immanent in all the universe, that God is the basis and the background of all that is manifest and existent.

Therefore, the wise man, the man of superior knowledge, the man of divine Knowledge, prays by way of his continued inner mental awareness of God everywhere. In all that is limited, he is conscious of the Unlimited. In all that is changing, he perceives the Unchanging. In all that is perishing, he discovers the Imperishable. He knows that every moment of time is being supported by the Timeless.

He penetrates into the phenomenon of life and discovers therein the seeds of the immortal Life. This is his prayer, his form of reflection, his type of dynamic and operative knowledge. That wise man whose intelligence touches the infinite and the absolute Principle wherever it is operating, can be best described as a man of prayer.

Seek the Infinite,
for that alone
is Joy unlimited, imperishable,
unfailing, self-sustaining,
unconditioned, timeless.
When you have this Joy,
the Light, the Grace,
the Power, the Perfections
of your supreme inner Consciousness
appear in your outer everyday life.

Swami Omkarananda

Mantra and Mystical Consciousness

God is there with You, whether You Are Conscious of Him or Not

Outside the unchanging Truth, outside the inseparable, all-wonderful God, there can be no peace, no joy, no strength, no life possible. You try to be a billionaire, and see if you can really find any peace, or happiness, or true life. You try to do what you may in the world and possess what you like in the world – through that there is no chance of your having any true peace, or true happiness, or true power, or true knowledge, or true life. Therefore, instead of wasting time in pursuing these things, get back to the unlimited Power, unlimited Happiness, unlimited Peace, unlimited Life, eternal Life, that God is. And in order to get back to God you need not to move even a metre. He is there where you are sitting. He is within you and around you; you have not seen Him.

A great cinema actress in Paris had a wonderful, very costly, expensive, three million dollar chain of diamonds. One day, in her excitement, she absent-mindedly put her chain round her neck and began to search for it. And in her big house and among her many servants she made such a chaos, thinking that it is lost, thinking that she has misplaced it somewhere in the house and the servants have stolen it. She made a great disorder in the whole house. She sent her servant maids searching for it. She telephoned to the police. She created a great chaos in her restlessness to find the necklace. Several hours were lost in this. At the end, one among the wise and calm persons of the household asked, *"Where did you last keep it?"*

"Well, it was in my dressing room."

"Did someone enter your dressing room?"

She said, *"No one except myself."*

And the wise man said, *"Good. Take off your mantle. What is there around your neck?"*

She was astonished to find, that the necklace was all the time there, and the scarf was hiding it! She was searching, suspecting the servants, accusing them, telephoning to the police. All the time the necklace was there around her neck.

Even so, all the time the necklace of billions of dollars, the necklace of infinite Happiness, Peace, Joy, Power, Grace, Beauty, Perfection, is around every man's neck. Not knowing this, every man is restlessly searching for pleasure, in the cinema, in the restaurant, with people. People are trying to cheat, deceive, in search of happiness, destroy other nations, grapple for the wealth of other countries, kill each other for a little power and a little wealth. All this human drama of restless chaos, disorder, sufferings, sorrow, injustice, evil is enstaged in search of pleasure and power and peace which no man finds. While all the time, around their necks there is the God of infinite Peace, Happiness, Power, true Love, true Freedom, true Grace. Remember this Truth. Do all you can to relate yourself to the Kingdom of Heaven, to God who is within you. And remember also the truth, outside this God you cannot find any true Wealth, true Peace, true Freedom, true Happiness, true Power, true eternal Life.

Mantra Repetition as a Powerful Means of Being in Tune with the Infinite

So long as the mind persists in any form, so long as the mind persists as your body, as the world around you, as your name, as your experiences, as your thoughts and feelings, as your awareness of the earth underneath, there is no true experience of God. When your mind becomes of the nature of God and ceases to be the body that you are, the world that you experience around you, then you have God-experience. The mind must forget itself, forget itself as your body, as the earth underneath, as everything that you see and know and experience in the outer world, as your thoughts and feelings. The moment mind ceases to be so, and assumes the form and nature of the heart of the Divine, it becomes divine, it has a true experience of God. Till then you have no true experience of God; you have the experience of anything else, but not of God. So in order there may be a true experience of God, your mind must cease to be aware of yourself as "so and so", your mind has to cease to be aware of the earth beneath and the environment around and must subsist as a boundless Light, Love, Grace and divine Consciousness.

The moment the pure in heart sit for meditation, they do not know that there is the earth underneath them, or people around them. No other thoughts are arising: the consciousness is immediately absorbed in the Infinite.

The mantra repetition is a powerful means of being in tune with this infinite and absolute God. The simple Saints go on saying millions of times during the day, *"God, God, God."* And thus they secure for themselves the experience of only one Thing: *"God, God, God."*

The normal man is completely lost in hundreds of silly experiences. Therefore, the normal man is so ignorant and morally imperfect, unhappy and restless, always seeking for goals which are never fulfilled. Your heart has also said millions of times: *"My body, my things, your body, your things, my father, my mother, my children, my typewriter, my happiness, my unhappiness, my salad, my chocolate."* Millions of times this is going on in the unconscious, and therefore you are tied to the earth. When the opposite process is started, you are liberated, spiritually freed and enlightened. You must say millions of times, *"God, God, God"*, in order that all these dirty experiences and impressions are effaced.

Mind is so treacherous that it makes us always forget God, and it makes us experience only a sensuous, physical, material world. Mind is completely absorbing us in a physical, earthly experience of pains and pleasure, good and bad; it is not allowing us to get closer to God. Therefore, we must discover special ways by which we can make the mind always think of God. In order to do that, supposing if you have a word like *"OM"*, or if you have a word like *"Lord"*, every time you say *"OM"* or *"Lord"*, you are reminded of God. And remember, the greatest Mystics and Saints have discovered that this OM is one and the same with God; and hundreds of Saints have had the vision of God. If that is so, why don't you try to control the mind and constantly put it in memory of God by repetition of the word *"OM"* or *"Lord"*?

Suppose, you are Mrs. Smith. You don't like Mrs. Brown. The moment you see Mrs. Brown, there are in you deep feelings of dislike for her. If you see her, you think of her daughter who offended you, and so on. So long as you are lost in this kind of experience, where is God in your life? On the other hand, with one word, *"OM"* or *"Lord"*, you can bring down God into your everyday existence. The moment you see Mrs. Brown, don't recognize her as Mrs. Brown; let all your heart and mind say: *"Lord"*. Now there is no more any feeling of hatred for Mrs. Brown, no more memory of her daughter's offending you. And there is a constant consciousness that God is omniscient, all-powerful, all-beautiful, that He is all-loving, all-seeing, that He is in Mrs. Brown and in yourself also. So instead of mind displaying the reactions of hatred, dislike, in the presence of Mrs. Brown, with that wonderful word *"Lord"* or *"OM"* it is full of a reflection upon God's Omniscience, Omnipotence, Protection, Beauty, Love, Light. So in this way you see how very valuable such a word, a mantra, is for daily life.

You see a car flying by. The moment you see it, you say *"God"*. That seeing the car becomes an excuse for remembering God, repeating God's name and submerging yourself in God-Consciousness. And instead of the car leaving an impression upon your mind, the emotion and awareness of God's presence remains in the mind the moment you repeat *"God"*.

Thus, you can apply the Lord's name everywhere, in all conditions of life, in all experiences, and in all situations. If you are going from one town to the other with the train, don't put your leg into the carriage until you say mentally or with all your heart, *"God"*. And don't sit down without uttering in your heart *"God"*, and experiencing the Lord's presence. If in the interval you get up from the seat for a minute, say *"God"*, and get up. And if the people around you in the carriage are constituting a distraction upon your eyes, you can pretend to be tired and close your eyes, and having closed your eyes again mentally and by heart say *"God"*. And you know what God is – an omnipresent, omnipotent, all-beautiful, all-protecting, all-seeing Power and Presence.

There are many types of mantras. The kind of mantra you repeat depends upon the kind of conception you have of God and the way you love Him. Mantra can be a verse, or it can be one mystical syllable like OM, or it can be a name of God; and the mantra has to be repeated again and again, until the mind is controlled, transformed, uplifted, united with God.

Mantras like OM are fundamental sounds, mystical sounds. They are not words created by man; they are not sounds caused, formed, created by the genius of man. Man, in his genius, has created many languages. All communications have been rendered possible by special languages he has evolved, but OM and other mystical syllables consist of sounds which are eternal, timeless, uncreated. Whereas there are other mantras which are created by the holiness and the divinity of an aspiring soul. They too are called mantras, because they, in the long run, lead one to God-experience.

The Supreme Mantra "OM"

OM is the supreme mantra, highest mantra. It is prefixed to every other mantra. It is the battery; if you put it in anything it becomes light. Add to the OM names of God, and it becomes a mantra.

When you are constantly repeating it, and all your heart and mind is in it, and through it you have spiritual experience, it is your mantra. If through its instrumentality you have God-experience, it becomes a mantra.

So mantra is the means by which you commune with the Divinity. Mantra is that by which you call upon the Divinity and ask It to be with you, in you, around you, in your experience. Mantra is something that holds your heart in Light, inspiration. Mantra purifies the mind, elevates the mind, makes the mind one-pointed; and from there you can meditate better. It also gives you strength in time of fear and distress. It also helps you see things clearly, mentally, in thought and in judgement, in times of doubt and difficulties.

Supposing your greatest friend suddenly enters into the room, how will you feel? Suddenly you jump out of the chair. Your face is full of smiles, and you warmly try to shake hands and embrace the friend. In the same way, always feel yourself suddenly in the presence of Someone called your greatest Friend: God. As your heart jumps into smiles and makes you embrace the friend, when you think of God let your heart jump with smiles, and embrace God's Presence. Every time you say the mantra let this experience be undergone. God is the greatest Reality – more real than the bones in your fingers – and is with you, around you, listening to you always.

So mantra is not merely a verbal repetition. It is being accompanied by love for God, faith in God, a perception which is in itself purifying you, transforming you, changing you, altering you radically within. When you are in the mantra, whatever nonsense you have heard, nothing has entered you. When you are in the mantra, whatever pains are experienced in the body, they have not touched you. When you are in the mantra, whatever may be the hundred limitations and weaknesses you have, they have not affected you. And when you are in this state, day after day, and year after year, nothing will any more trouble you: you are all-perfect. You are as perfect as the Divine.

OM is a divine Word, the Word of God, that was in the beginning and that will be at the end, that is always in the universe, that is always in your inner spiritual heart. All the highest mysteries of the infinite Consciousness, the potentialities and powers of absolute Consciousness are resident in OM. Therefore, It is something which constitutes the key to the whole reality of the Infinite.

OM is that fundamental Sound which has brought into existence all forms of sounds, all types and frequencies of sound. It is the Energy behind all energies. It is the Infinite. It has brought into existence time and space, and in the time- and space-universe It is resident. Resident in it, It is yet exceeding it.

The beautiful tree that you see with its green leaves and beautiful flowers and fruits is also a product of OM, is being sustained in its energy by OM. The life in the tree by which the tree grows is a product of OM and is sustained by OM.

So OM is the pervasive, all-permeating Energy in the universe. It is the Music of the celestial spheres that is in all the magnificent activity of the stellar universes beyond and the fundamental, all-pervasive, all-creating Force, the Force which is the basis and foundation even of consciousness and intelligence and awareness, the Force which bears all magnetism. All forces like the gravitational force, even powers like the power of love and faith, are energies, forces, emanating from the universal, all-pervading OM.

This grand, infinite Being that OM is, has not only brought into existence, by the million energies in Its Being, this universe, but It is also something transcendent and exceeding and standing beyond what It has created.

Now, how to understand this much better? Take the case of our own mind. Can you see what mind is? Nobody knows what mind is – not your greatest psychologist. He can frighten you by special cases, published by the world-leading universities, but he is a poor fool, a child, playing tricks. Nobody knows what mind is, what its nature is. Let us take a hypothesis. Let us consider mind as something like an atom, an electronic atom in our brains. Let us say it is a tiny little particle of light in our brains. We fall asleep. Now the body is at complete rest, the mind's activities are completely suspended, we are not conscious of the body or the external world, we don't know what time it is, we don't know that we are sleeping. All this knowledge is blocked out; we are in a deep darkness; we are in deep sleep. Suddenly a dream arises. You feel that it is 9 o'clock. There is a blazing sun. You feel that you are in a tropical forest in Africa. You feel that you are a young person, aged 20 years, a man. You experience that you are walking along a path in the forest. There is a terrific glare of the blazing sun. You find the deer and some animals of the forest crossing your path. In the meantime, something awakens you from the sleep. Your dream is broken.

Now you are, say, a woman. You had a dream. In that dream you felt that you were a boy walking in the blazing sun at 9 o'clock on the path in a South African forest. Who created that boy? Who created that sun in the dream, that forest, those animals which you saw? This fantastic mind in you, which is just this tiny little thing in your brain, in your head, had created a sun, a world, the sunshine, the animals, the huge forest. This tiny little space in the head which does not hold even a single tree, could hold the whole forest, could give you experiences which embrace vast spaces.

All these experiences you had within your brain, within your mind, within such a short time. Was not that boy you saw and felt yourself to be in the dream purely a creation of your mind? Was not that person formed of the substance of your mind? Were not that sun, those forests, the trees that you saw all formed by the mind? And as you were walking as that young man, and while all the time thinking that you are different and distinct from whatever you have been experiencing in that forest, was not all this a possibility, a grand self-expression of the power of the mind in you? Was not, in everything that you saw, the central mind's capacity and energy present, pervasive?

Even so, OM, which is a tiny little Particle, has brought into existence all these vast and immeasurable spaces of the universe, all this creation, and all that time that accompanies the processes of this universal being. All these have emerged from that tiny little OM.

What is this tiny Thing which is infinite in Its expression? That is why a passage in the Upanishad says, God, the supreme Reality, is smaller than the smallest particle, and vaster than the infinite space. Is this not a paradox? How can the smallest, the tiniest thing, which is smaller than the smallest atom, be, at the same time, vaster, greater than the vast, immeasurable space which cannot be measured even by light-years? It is not a paradox for those who have direct experience of God.

OM is both, God as impersonal and transcendental, and God as immanent and personal. It combines both aspects of God.

OM is divine Harmony. It is divine Consciousness. It is divine Intelligence. Its very nature is Luminosity. It is indescribably brilliant. Its nature is also Love. It is infinite and boundless Love. Its nature is also Beauty. It is Fullness. It is infinite and absolute Peace. It is the Music of music. It is absolute Joy. It is everything, and transcends everything. OM contains in Itself the manifest and the unmanifest aspects of the Divine.

Every repetition of OM should help your mind and heart suddenly touch something of God's Presence, Power, Light. Every repetition of OM should be for you a means of establishing active relations with God. Let every repetition of OM be accompanied by the knowledge that It is the Word of God, and God is in It, that It is of God, that It is God's sound-form. Let every hair and foot and tooth, everything, repeat the mantra, let everything repeat the mantra. Take it into the subconscious. Take the mantra into the unconscious. Take the mantra into the conscious memory, and so on. Every part and portion of your inner being and consciousness must be charged with the mantra power.

You must repeat the mantra, not mechanically, but with a feeling, awareness, that the Divinity is present with you, around you. When you are repeating the mantra, if you are full of faith and love for the Divine, if you are conscious that God is omnipotent, omnipresent, omniscient, if you know that there is Someone who loves you supremely, Someone who is your beloved, Someone who is your strength and support and life, the Divinity, all-seeing, all-powerful, all-wonderful, eternal, and that we cannot separate ourselves from It – such a Divinity is with you.

When you meditate and find peace in meditation, and also a sense of God's Consciousness, you can bring that peace and God-consciousness into your work through the help of this word OM. Whenever you say

OM, let peace be poured into your mind and heart and will, and let peace express itself through your outer actions. So through continuous repetition of OM you will be able to sustain yourself in peace and God-inspiration.

Whenever peace or inspiration or God-consciousness wanes, at once repeat OM, loudly or mentally or by heart. When the OM is chanted, it releases such a fire and force and energy that harmonizes the atmosphere around us, that drives away and destroys discordant forces around us. Repeat for fifteen minutes. As you repeat, disturbing thoughts and feelings subside. And with every repetition feel that you are in the immediate presence of God, that OM is God, that God is expressing Himself through OM, that this mantra is the means of your establishing relations with God. And wherever OM is repeated, there God's presence is at once generated: there, at once the obstacles and the veils that are hiding God's presence from your view are broken.

The Powers of the Mind in God-Consciousness

Men of highest God-experience are always listening to the OM sound everywhere in the universe. Put your ear to the telegraph post; you will hear a sound. In the same way, the whole world is resonating, all the universes are resonant, with this fundamental sound OM.

The human ear is so gross and so limited that it cannot hear finer and higher sounds, but in the state of mystical consciousness and God-experience, they are disclosed to the Super-Scientists that the greatest Sages are.

Why do I say these Mystics and Sages are Super-Scientists? In the textbooks of science, books that relate to sound phenomena, you might have learned there are frequencies of sound which are inaudible to the ear. There are delicate sounds which our ear cannot catch. There are terrific sounds which also our ear does not catch. Our ear is capacitated to catch only those sounds which fall within a certain specific, small, tiny band. This poor human ear of ours is a petty power, a useless thing, useful only for conducting an animal existence, but not useful for higher purposes. So the scientist governed and guided by a spirit of search for more knowledge, devoted to discovery of facts, laws, truths of physical things, has been studying the phenomena of sound in the laboratory.

Now, by the fruitfulness of these marvellous researches, experiments, and by a combination of several technological factors, the modern scientist has helped us to have what you call hearing-aids, has made for us the radio, transistor, and so on. And this radio catches those sound-waves, which are inaudible to the physical ear. The radio catches these sound-waves of all frequencies and amplifies these sounds in order that our ear may catch them. From this we understand our physical ears are extremely limited in their capacity for hearing sounds.

It is also possible to hear the radio-waves and frequencies without the aid of the radio-apparatus. The Sage and Mystic is sitting with us, and the news broadcasted by BBC in London is heard by Him, though He has no radio apparatus. Is not the brain of this Mystic more marvellous than the radio? He can tune Himself to any station while sitting here. Is not His brain super-scientific? He can not only tune Himself to any radio-station, but He can tune Himself to a man in Bern, Switzerland, and report what is happening in his head, what he is thinking. He can also tune Himself to anyone in some corner in any city in Australia, and immediately give the whole story of their activities right from the morning till now.

You have a television. When you turn to a particular station, you see the whole picture, the whole story unfolded. Whereas this Sage can see any street, any house, in any city of the world. Suppose, war is taking place in South Vietnam. Cables are received by newspaper offices in London, in Paris, in Zurich, and all over the world, concerning the happenings on the field of war. But the Sage who is sitting here, with us, is a direct witness to what is happening there. Is not this Sage's mind far more marvellous than the most marvellous scientific apparatus that television is? Can you not therefore call Him a Super-Scientist?

Your mind is limited in its powers. You do not even know what Mrs. Herrmann is thinking now, you do not even know what is happening deep down in her subconscious and unconscious. You do not know what is going to happen to you tomorrow. Whereas this Saint's and Mystic's mind is unlimited, timeless, spaceless in its function and power. Therefore, He can also tell you, and present picture for picture, what happened 5000 years ago in the place where the city of Zurich now stands, how it looked like, how the people dressed themselves, how they lived and ate and drank, and the complete life-story of any one of them.

The mind of the Saint can travel back in time, or travel ahead in time, or make all space an immediate here. If scientists are struggling hard to fly to the moon, yet the knowledge that they have acquired concerning the moon is inadequate, insufficient; their efforts are not successful. But the Saint looks at the moon as if you are looking at a ball on this table – not only at the moon, but at any planet. For Him there are no spatial limitations. His mind is moving in a spaceless, timeless universe.

Science tells us that if a star dies somewhere it takes millions and millions and millions of light-years before its light arrives here on earth. Whereas the mind of the Sage, in half a split second, is by the star. That means the mind of the Sage is moving at a terrific speed, at which light cannot travel. His consciousness is the Light behind all lights. Space, time, all are meaningless for Him.

He is living in the world of real marvels and wonders of divine Consciousness. He has not only access to this world of time and space, this physical universe; He has also access to all the invisible mental worlds, psychic worlds, spiritual worlds. So He can penetrate into the minds of humanity, live in and know directly all the worlds. He can move into the other higher worlds, heaven or hell, or whatever may be, as easily as you move from one room of your house into the next one. Such is the state of the mind achieved in Illumination; such are the powers of the mind in God-consciousness.

Now if a Mystic were to put His ear to the tree, He will hear the sound of OM, the fundamental Sound. If He looks at the universe, He is conscious of the vibrations of OM sustaining, maintaining, forming that universe. All that He sees, knows, feels through the senses is found to be formulations of this fundamental divine Consciousness, Energy, Force. So the Mystic is not only conscious of God in the universe, in the space-time-universe, but also is conscious of God beyond the universe.

The Mystical Powers of the Mantra

How can we ourselves achieve this state of the Mystic? You know, as science tells you, that tremendous energy, inconceivable energy, is locked up in the tiny little atom. Science says: *"Split that atom, and you will release terrific atomic energy, sufficient to destroy cities, or sufficient to put a number of factories at work."* In the same way, mantra is that power, which splits the atom of our inner consciousness. Go on splitting the inner atom of the consciousness;

tomorrow you yourself will become this Super-Scientist that the Sage or Mystic is.

You see the point? The scientists are splitting the material atoms. The material atoms are inferior, infinitely inferior to the atom of consciousness. What happens when you go on splitting the atoms of consciousness by the mystic power that mantra is? After some years, your own mind will be full of millions of television- and radio-sets and millions of kingdoms of heaven. Your joy will be so great that you cannot imagine it. Your peace will be so much that nobody can understand it, a joy that is indescribable, as the Veda says. You will be living in a self-sufficient, self-contained world. This is your real destiny.

Wherever the Sage is, there inside his being is the Kingdom of Heaven. Now supposing this city is going to be bombed, the government at once announces: *"Walk out of the city!"* All are frightened. The Sage is simply sitting, smiling. You understand? What can attempt to catch this person, who is a super-atom?

Now there is a blazing fire. In that blazing fire, if you put a cup of water, what does it do? It only evaporates in the fire. So, when you yourself become a super-atom, there is no fear. You become absolutely fearless; you will be smiling; there is no such thing as danger. When you are brought face to face with a dozen lions, you will still be smiling; they are tiny cats for you – more afraid of you, and more happy in your presence, and incapable of mischief in your presence. Why? Because the vibrations of your personality affect them, touch them.

There are beautiful rose plants. You are not seeing them, but their fragrance is reaching us, and we suspect there is some rose plant somewhere there. In the same way, everything is emanating its own fragrance and its own vibration. Now you have sandalwood; it is emanating a fragrant smell. In the same way, all of us, all of our bodies, our minds and personalities, are emanating vibrations. How much more elevated, happy, inspired in the presence of a Holy Personality we feel! We feel in His presence God-realization is an easy matter. We feel in His presence life's difficulties are nothing. If an evil person is there, he feels somehow depressed; automatically he feels slightly uneasy. He will say, *"Let us go for a walk!"*

So all of us are emanating our own vibrations. We are constantly radiating specific energies; they are good or bad in accordance with the goodness or badness of our minds and hearts.

So when you are repeating the mantra, all the negative, dark vibrations, energies in you, are becoming illuminated, you are being transformed inside, a spiritual power is being generated in you. This spiritual power is felt by all sensitive minds that come into contact with you. If you go to a sick man he feels enlivened, he feels inspired, he feels that he will recover soon, he feels he is happy and he can manage and everything will be all right.

So I say, go on repeating your mantra. You will release wonderful vibrations. Your very car will draw, suck in your vibrations, and if there were to be an accident for the car it would miraculously escape it, because the vibrations will not allow any damage to take place.

Every time you are repeating the mantra you are releasing specific, definite vibrations, of which you may not be conscious, but whose results and effects you can always notice and see in what is happening around you and in your life.

A heart of compassion and universal Love
will unfold from within you,
the divine Kingdom of Illumination.
Love is Light, and Light is Illumination.

The road to Enlightenment
lies through acts of universal Love.

A life of humility and unconditional love
born of purity of nature,
God-knowledge and communion with God
through prayer and meditation,
fills you with Divine Grace and Light
which in turn,
will so fully illuminate your inner being,
that you begin to behold the Splendour of God
everywhere.

It is then,
that all the riddles of life are resolved,
and the darkness of limited life's
confusing and difficult circumstances
completely dispelled.

Swami Omkarananda

The Wonders of Love

Love is Greater than Wisdom, Logic, Virtue and Prayer

More than intelligence, Love quickens talent and genius. Without Love, intelligence can do much harm. More than logic, Love assigns to reason the dignity of an unerring thought. Without Love, logic can be dangerous.

More than Law, Love dispenses a justice that elicits ultroneously the enthusiastic approval of Man, God and all Nature. Without Love, law can be blind and cruel.

More than wisdom, Love is an all-comprehending Virtue, and spans in the extent of its phenomenon, meaning and power, both the ethical and the spiritual thought, action and achievement. There can be no real wisdom, without Love. Love is a Power for accomplishment, a Force for culture, a Sentiment that renders all life, one. Love is an exalted emotion that uplifts the soul of man into a divine Awareness.

More than prayer, Love unites the soul of man with God. Without Love, prayer can be less than useless, and ineffective. Love is everything. Blessed is thy Heart of Love. Spread the sunshine and smiles of thy Love everywhere, in your own gentle and silent way!

Science in Future will Establish the Psychosomatic Value of Love

Extending its researches into the dynamism of the psychosomatic phenomenon, the modern Mind would one day establish as a scientific fact that as yet little-known truth, that Love sweetens saliva, kills the bad germs in the system, oxygenates the blood, purifies the whole organism. Love is the chief solvent of the several ills to which human individual is a heir. The medicinal value and therapeutic utility of Love, cannot be exaggerated.

Above all, Love is to be considered as the highest technique for spiritual realization.

Your Love Contains Hundred Virtues

The single element of Love in your blessed heart contains hundred virtues. The grand, deep, wide, divine Love in your heart, forgives. Love is charitable. Love judges not. Love resists not evil. Love is a peacemaker. Love is humble and self-giving. Thanks to your all-encompassing and unfailing Love! Let its dimensions expand more, and gain for you the highest State of God-experience.

The Modern Religion of Love

God is Love: therefore, religion ceases to be religion, if it is not a religion of love. Love understands, knows, illuminates, conquers and makes life eternal. Love purifies and liberates. Love is to be known and experienced by love. Since God is Love, the way to Him, is through Love.

Love of God is the soul of religion. It annihilates all limitations and differentiations. It frees human perception from its errors, human heart from its mistakes and human life from its imperfections.

From the lover of God, Love streams forth equally to all beings, even as the warmth streams forth from the sun, equally to all. It is the potent remedy for curing the disease of fear, hatred, discord, unhappiness.

Pure love is an irresistible force. To him whose heart is filled with pure love, the voice of his own conscience is the voice of God. He engages himself in alleviating the suffering of others. His is an ideal of selfless service. God's will works through him. God's Light shines through him. God's Life expresses itself through him. Ever joyful and fearless, he brings into the life of anyone he comes across, peace, harmony, strength, happiness.

The religion of pure Love is the only real foundation of the lasting unity of all humanity. With such a religion alone life becomes a song of peace, progress, perfection, and the world a heaven.

Love is Everything

The best description of the Being of God, is Love. Love is the soul of all Nature, and the Divinity in Man. Love is the highest Good, the Highest Truth and the highest Beauty, and it unites in itself the basic processes of the three normative sciences, ethics, logic, and aesthetics. Love is the supreme virtue. It is the mainspring of all other virtues.

Our View of Virtue as Love

Intellectualistic in ethics, Socrates conceives of virtue as knowledge. Seeking to improve upon the Socratic rational insight by introducing into it a volitional element, Aristotle conceives of virtue as the right willing, the choice of the mean. Our view of virtue as Love includes, as integral to itself, the Socratic knowing, the Aristotelian willing, and exceeds and corrects them by a great comprehensiveness. An exclusive preoccupation with the art, the understanding, the advocacy and the achievement of the excellent in the merely cultural refinement, ruled out from the Hellenic ideal of character, the element of Love. Without Love we can conceive of no Saint, think of no spiritual realization, build no genuine social harmony and human unity. With love alone, there is the possibility of a deep and elemental psychic and divine experience.

Love and Knowledge Illuminate Life

The first and last aim of life on earth is the obtainment of real Knowledge, Love, Peace, Happiness, higher Powers, Freedom, Immortality. But, this obtainment can be had only by one way; there is no other way. It is the way of the unfoldment of the highest divine Consciousness within us, the way of God-Experience. This divine experience is possible by an increasing knowledge of the ultimate Ground of our existence, God, and an increasing love for the absolute value that Ground bears in itself. Therefore, it is the way of Knowledge and Love. We are safe only on this way. Only by Knowledge and Love, we grow. The most wonderful persons in the world are wonderful because they have Love and Knowledge. You too are wonderful because of your Love and Knowledge.

The Rights of Man to Happiness, Love, Power and Life

There is none, no man, however evil, sinful and abandoned, who is not, in some corner of his being, splendidly good and, in some inmost and secret recess of his consciousness, truly divine, and, in his awakened hours, fully aware that he had adopted wrong means to arrive at what is the legitimate right of his birth into the world, the right for Happiness, infinite Happiness, endless Happiness, for Freedom, infinite Freedom, endless Freedom, for Power, infinite Power, endless Power, for Love, infinite Love, endless Love, for Life, infinite Life, endless Life.

And so long as Man is Man, however supremely good, or extremely evil, he would have moments in which he is bound to gaze on the luminous person of a God-incarnation, or recollect calmly the sublimity and pertinence of His teaching, or derive from a thought devoted to Him, the needed inspiration. Man is a son of God and the outer shell of his evil will break.

Examine the Foundations of Your Love

Be kind to animals; it is good. Love all; it is good, but do not get emotionally involved in anything. Emotional attachment will take away your peace of mind, will deprive you of your freedom to grow further, and will impair the sight of your reason. Therefore, found your kindness and your love first upon the Knowledge of the divine Existence and Consciousness, God, present in the inner heart of all beings. Love everything, not for small reasons which change, not for the exteriors which alter, not under circumstances which disappear, but for the sake of the Life, the Godhead, in all beings. Such a love is the love of wisdom, a pure love, unfailing and never troubled Love.

Real Love, its Nature and its Power

Love brings and enriches love. Love does not rest content with merely loving, but flows out in acts of service. Love is delightful only when it freely gives itself. Love must be revealed in service; otherwise, love has no value; such a love is no love. Love cheerfully sacrifices. Love willingly suffers. Such a love illumines and blesses life. Love for God, real devotion, is not mere emotionalism, it is the tuning of the will, the heart and the mind to the eternal and indestructible Music of the Divine. It blossoms into Wisdom divine. It leads to God-Experience and attainment of Immortality.

Our Blessings from Divine Love

We are full of peace, because our inner being has its intimate relations in love with that which is infinitely peaceful, – God. We are happy, because our hearts are in tune with that which is infinite Delight, – God. We are strong, because we are in constant relations with that which is Omnipotent. We are wise, because our intelligence is submitted to the guidance of the all-seeing, all-knowing Consciousness of the Supreme Being. We are loving, because we experience in the inner being of all, the Presence of the all-lovable Godhead. We are energetic and hard-working, because we have the joy of dedicating all our works to the advancement of Peace, Prosperity, Knowledge, Happiness, in this good world that God made.

How to Love God?

Love God with all thy heart, and thy neighbour as thy own inner divine Self. This is the way of the Saints. This is religion. When we love God with all our heart, all our soul, all our might, day after day, day and night, for months and for years, we arrive at a stage of development where we experience God everywhere, at all times, and in all circumstances and environs.

How to Develop Love for God?

Keep company of the good, the noble, and the pure. Contact the Saints. Their exalted and impressive lives, and their inspiring speech, will awaken your spiritual sensibilities and the dormant love for God, in your heart. Control your emotional nature, refine your intelligence, and sublimate and transform your psychological nature. Your love for God will grow. Develop your moral nature, the spirit of service and sacrifice. Your love for God will grow. Study the descriptions of the Nature of God presented by those who have had an intimate experience of God. Your love for God will grow.

How to Love the Neighbour as Thyself?

Do you not wish to yourself happiness, peace, success and well-being? Then, wish these to everybody. Do you wish to be hurt or insulted? Then, hurt or insult no one. Do you not wish to be liked, respected and loved? Then, like, respect and love others. Do you not desire freedom to do what you like in all your ways? Then, give complete freedom to others. Do you not like the full joy of living? Then, help others find the full joy of living. Do you wish someone to speak ill of you? Then, speak ill of no one. First, give to everyone just that which you wish to have from them. This is the way to love the neighbour as thyself.

What is Higher Love?

Higher Love is unconditioned goodwill. A will which never, under no conditions, wishes anybody harm, a will which expresses for all people, at all times, and without any compromise, peace, happiness, health and welfare, – that is higher Love. It is the exalted inner perception of the union with the imperishable and all-sustaining divine Being in all that which is manifest.

How to Love All Humanity?

Close your eyes for a half a minute, and wish welfare for all humanity. Generate loving and kind thoughts for all beings. Say: *"May all be happy, may none on earth be unhappy."* Say: *"Peace to all corners of the world, and to all beings."* Let there be no hatred of any kind in your heart for anyone.

Wish victory to the forces of Goodness, Truth, Love, Godliness, Justice, in the world; and all those people and those nations, which embody these, will prosper.

This heart of all-inclusive Love, extended by a few moments of silence, prayer and contemplation, – this is universal Love; this is the way to love all beings, all over this vast world.

Everybody is your friend,
when your heart throbs with friendly feelings.
Where there is the warmth of real love
in your heart,
your eyes are luminous, your face declares it,
and your behaviour expresses it,
and you get friends unasked.

When you obey laws of health,
your body is your friend.
When you love God, Nature is your friend.
When you love man, God is your friend.
When you love hard work, success is your friend.
When you possess an understanding heart,
peace and harmony are your friends.
When you love fresh air, cleanliness, good habits,
radiant health is your friend.
When you love the development of your intelligence
and the growth of your faith,
Illumination is your friend.

Everywhere you have a friend.
In all things there is a friend for you.

Swami Omkarananda

The Good Heart

The good heart is the greatest treasure of the human individual. It understands, loves, forgives, and is cheerfulness. It has nobility, generosity, and embodies in itself faith, devotion, trust, and several other life-enriching and illuminating virtues.

With a good heart, the poor man is a very rich man; without it, a rich man is a very poor man.

With it, a doctor, or a priest, is a Saint; without it, a political or religious leader, is a creator of battles, discord and unhappiness.

With a good heart, the mother is a queen. Without it, a queen is the mother of the misfortune of millions of people. With it, a woman is a Goddess, and therefore, really beautiful. Without it, life is a vale of gloom and despair.

The good heart can make a Heaven of hell, Peace of war, Joy of misery. It is the maker of the perpetual sunshine.

Just see what one of the world's greatest poets, William Shakespeare, has to say with regard to a good heart, in his work, Henry V, 5,2:

"A good leg will fall, a straight back will stoop, a black beard will turn white, a curled pate will grow bald, a fair face will wither, a full eye will wax hollow; but a good heart

is the sun and the moon; or, rather the sun and not the moon; for, it shines bright and never changes, but keeps his course truly."

What is Good?

Good is anything that grants you health, strength, peace of mind, happiness and intense God-Consciousness.

All that develops your abilities, capacities, excellences, all that gives you mastery over yourself and your environment, conditions, circumstances, and liberates you from every form of slavery, – slavery to urges and impulses from within you, or to objects and things outside you, – is good.

When something is done, if there ensues as our personal inner experience, joy, exhilaration or satisfaction, we can understand that we are doing a right action; but, if there arises in us a sense of uneasiness, fear, shame, doubt, or pricking of conscience, we must recognize it to be a wrong action.

Ultimately, all actions which contribute to our inner moral and spiritual development and take us closer to our experience of God and our achievement of divine Perfection, are the best.

Evil Cannot Subsist

Evil cannot subsist, the moment you do not fear it, stop paying attention to it, withdraw your will from it, and refuse to accept it. The moment you are occupied with something absolutely positive and grand, with something that promotes your development, evil loses its power.

With the all-conquering positive attitude, you are able to meet any situation in life, any bad person, any evil condition, or experience, find much peace, joy, power, and gain the capacity to make a true heaven of your life.

The Test of Our Goodness

To anything or any person, there are always more than a dozen views or attitudes that we can take. Select that view or that attitude which is the best. The choice we make bears witness to the stage of our development and evolution. The better the attitude, the quicker would be our progress to the next stage of development. And the attitude we take settles our own greatness or meanness.

The nobler the nature, the nobler the attitude. Nothing tests our goodness so well, or publicizes our nature so ably, as the view or the attitude we adopt from among the many possible views and attitudes to anything or any person.

How to Do the Right Thing

It is not right to do a thing that

a) troubles your conscience, causes regret and any form of fear in you; or
b) is disapproved by the voice of that which is best and highest in you; or
c) disturbs your mental peace; or
d) weakens your nerves, takes away power from your will, and does not contribute to your real and lasting happiness; or
e) does not serve the interests of your mental, moral, cultural, spiritual growth and development.

Thanks to Your Magnanimity

Moralists must discern more in a magnanimous nature, even as the psychologists of human behaviour should widen their insights into those extra-ethical processes that engender the temper marked by modesty, by a noble restraint, a gracious reticence, a socially pleasing self-restraint. In action, expression and result, modesty is markedly individualistic, and magnanimity is more distinctly social, and cannot be manifest except as such, and what is more, on a deeper analysis, is seen to be supra-social in resources, nature and aims.

Magnanimity is the largeness of heart and greatness of soul. It is generosity in sentiment and nobility in conduct. A magnanimous person derives the power of his strong and attractive personality from total freedom from all kinds of meanness, selfishness, vindictive nature. Broad in outlook, liberal in views, lofty in character, the magnanimous person is an embodiment of good-will, self-sacrifice, courage, and moral uprightness.

Sympathy

Callousness finds a congenial soil in the heart that lacks, or loses, the capacity for sympathetic sensitiveness. If the spiritual individual, for purposes of a defence, and development, of the humaneness of humanity, is hard on anything, he is hard only on the granite heart. Scholars have always laboured under a tendency that permits the pre-eminence of the economist in Adam Smith, to obscure the importance of the ardent ethical theorist in him. Author of '*The Wealth of Nations*', he is also the author of '*The Theory of Moral Sentiments*', a work which preceded the former, furnished his name with a firm foundation for reputation, and contributed not unsubstantially to the studies in the science of ethics. In that book, Adam Smith seeks to make sympathy the fundamental fact of moral consciousness.

With the spiritual individual, sympathy is a universal solvent, and his statements, filled with sweetness, on this altruistic quality are always most eloquent.

To the minds that are inclined to perceive, or discover, or to comment upon, the possibilities, or actualities, of the relations in ethics, between theory and practice, it will be significant to note that the spiritual individual is seen, in his own life, to set no limits to his sympathies, and that their power is proved by the fact that they are accompanied by acts of loving kindness which are unnumbered.

Total Conquest of Anger Through Increasing Development of Inner Qualities

Goodness grants a serene mind and a cheerful spirit, which are, – better judgement argues – far more worthy of pursuit than all the pleasures in the world's greatest pleasure resorts. Where anger breaks things and suffers losses, patience bears things and wins victories. Impatience leads to loss of temper. Be patient like the earth, gentle like the breeze, forbearing like the tree, fragrant like the rose, sweet like the honey. Herein lies the road to a rich, grand, compelling and inspiring personality as also to the joy and the perfection of living.

Your Nobility and Royal Blood

The love that looks for a return, is a beggar. The kind act that turns back to see for a reward, is a shop-keeper who gives you nothing unless you pay for it. The person who stops praying because it was not answered, never knows what prayer is. The wife that guards herself in faithfulness, and suspiciously watches the faithfulness of her husband, lacks real love, cannot be faithful for long, and will make of the family a discordant phenomenon. To give, give more, freely, almost blindly, and not expect or ask, – this is real nobility. To take upon oneself suffering, in order to relieve others of suffering, – this is the spirit of the bearer of the real royal blood.

The Religion of Your Heart

That is Religion,

where the hands build,
where the heart loves,
where the life grows,
where the lips smile in goodness,
where the mind thinks noble thoughts,
where truth and honest labour produce a
heaven of peace,
where a song is made of home,
where the soul prays,
where faith knows the omnipresent God,
where man is in communion with
infinite Wisdom, Beauty, Light of God.

Such a religion is the religion of goodness in the heart of everyman made in the image of God.

The perception of
the one Life Principle or God,
in all,
the merging of the personal self
in the Divine Self
of all creatures, great and small,
is the ultimate meaning and end of life.
To rise from this world of limitations
while yet breathing on earth
into the boundless world
of Freedom and Beauty,
Power and Joy,
is the purpose of our brief,
but meaningful existence.

Swami Omkarananda

The Source of all Perfection

We are bearing the very Source of all Perfection, Beauty, Wisdom and Love within our own Self.

Unending Peace and Happiness are our own very nature.

Our own heart is the Sanctum Sanctorum, the Ocean of Nectar, the eternal abode of the Divinity.

Whichever desire may wake in a heart, it is just the desire for THIS.

But the curtain of ignorance separates us from this imperishable Reality.

Running after a world of vanishing values, pleasure and pain, we close our eyes for the indestructible, never changing, boundless Treasure of indescribable Beauty and Love, which is hidden in our own very Self. We are like a king that leaves his palace to search for rotten food on the dumping grounds.

As soon as realizing this, our heart loosens its grip on the desires for the illusionary world; we will experience a Peace and Bliss that can never be obtained by any sense pleasures.

Every phase of life has in it some poetry.
Every facet of life is aglow
with the eternal Energy and Light
of the infinite Truth.
Every circumstance of life is rich
with the splendour of spiritual glory.
The whole world is throbbing
with the divine Consciousness
that is the source, the soil and the fulfilment
of all that is.
Man's primary duty consists in knowing,
and being in harmony with,
this all-pervading, all-sustaining, infinite Light
of the
supreme Reality, Being, Existence, Consciousness.

Swami Omkarananda

The Message of the Omkarananda Upanishad

I do not occupy any space in the world. I am the only person, which is not on earth, not in time and space. I am not a burden for the earth. I do not occupy any spot in the space. Space is not burdened by me. I do not owe anything to space. I am no burden for the time.

Nobody and nothing should suffer because of me.

I am not there. In spite of that I am everywhere.

I have no weight. Everything in the world has weight – I am without weight.

I am dwelling in this Seer in me. I am dwelling in the Seer in you. This Seer does not occupy any space, does not need any space, is lighter than space.

Every form, even a feather, even a puff-ball* occupies the space, has weight. Light also has weight, form, but the Light that I am has no weight. It is timeless, it is spaceless, it is immeasurable.

Thoughts occupy space, feelings occupy space; feelings are objects like physical objects. Thoughts are objects. Everything occupies space of one kind or the other. In dream-experiences, dream-objects, dream-persons occupy dream space-time world.

---

* Puff-ball = seeds of the dandelion flower

I am the only person in all the worlds who occupies no time-space-order. If the space wants to see me, it can't, I am just not there. I am the Seer in the space, the space cannot see without me, yet I have no weight.

On the other hand, I support all space-time-orders. I am subtler than the subtlest thing. I am not a thing. I am so subtle, that nothing can see me, not the subtlest thing called space. I am infinitely subtler than space. I am infinitely smaller than the smallest pin-point you can think of.

I am at the same time greater and vaster than the vastest thing you can think of, the vastest thing that you can conceive of, be that the Absolute or the Infinite. I am greater than that, and without me you have no experience. All your experiences are founded on me. I am the Seer in you. I give light to your intelligence. You have no direct experience of anything in life outside me. Only concerning me you have a direct experience, for I am the Seer in you. There is nothing behind the Seer, before the Seer, above the Seer, below the Seer. The Seer is omnipresent. This Seer is the basis of all your experiences.

You have no direct experience of anything in life. How you experience the world outside your body? You scratch your skin with the nails of your fingers, it bleeds, it pains, you experience all this through senses, through intelligence, outer intelligence, physical intelligence, mental intelligence. You experience in this manner that is called "indirect experience". Every experience which is experienced through something is an indirect experience.

Supposing you were mad, insane, you do not experience the pain in the way a normal person experiences. Supposing you were unconscious, then you experience nothing. Supposing you are under chloroform, then also you experience nothing. Every kind of experience in your life is a mediate experience, indirect experience; only the Seer in you can have direct experience. All that is functioning in you subjectively and objectively is outside this Seer. That is all changing, passing. With none of your sense-organs you can see the Seer. Intelligence can see your thoughts inside your brain, subjective experiences. All these subjective experiences are experiences of your psychic and mental being. The Seer is seeing all this. The Seer is other than all this. All these pass away, change, are conditioned, give false knowledge. Sometimes, it is pleasant experience, sometimes it is unpleasant experience. The same thing gives sometimes pleasure, sometimes displeasure, unpleasantness. All these are outside the Seer. You experience everything inside and outside through some instrument, intelligence. If the intelligence is destroyed, you see two things where others see one thing. Every knowledge obtained through some medium is an indirect knowledge, and therefore can mislead you at one time or the other.

Everything is experienced through something else, whereas the Seer in you is alone experiencing directly.

The Seer is seeing your seeing intelligence. Your seeing intelligence is again an instrument. The moment you abandon your position in the seeing intelligence and sink into the Seer in you, even as you sink into this Seer during the deep-sleep state, then you have direct experience, there you experience without an instrument. It is non-mediate knowledge. It is direct knowledge. You have become that which you are experiencing. There is no medium here, no instrument here, you have become the Seer Himself. Only of this Seer you have direct knowledge. You become the Seer and be the Seer. This Seer I am in all things, in all beings. Therefore, only of me everyone can have direct knowledge.

I am subtler than space.

My nature is absolute Happiness. I occupy no space. All space is in me, without touching Me. This is a mystery. It is no mystery, if you understand the extremely subtle nature of my Being: the Seer that I am. It is so subtle that all that is happening within me, millions of universes, being sustained by it, in it, do not touch it. It is ever-pure, it is ever-perfect.

During the dream-state, you carry in your own head the whole universe, with all the rivers, all the seas or oceans, all the shining stars. Just imagine what the weight of a star is! And during this dream-experience everything therein is real. The star in the dream has the same weight as the star in the waking-life there in the sky, and the star is bigger perhaps than our sun. In spite of this bearing this whole universe in this brain during dream-state – do you feel any weight? Are you burdened by it? No. In the same way, the Seer in me is bearing all these rivers that you are seeing during the waking-state. Yet they have no weight in me, are no burden to me. And by their disappearance, they leave no trace on me, no scars.

This Being I am.

Anyone who wants to live a divine life must live in this Seer, in this Timelessness and Spacelessness, in this unlimited Joy, unlimited Peace, unlimited Perfection and Beauty. Anyone who lives outside this Seer is living a worldly life, a material life, a life that changes, a life that is attended with problems, questions, difficulties, oppositions.

Think of any most wonderful life you want to live, just bring the picture of the most extraordinary life you want to live, the happiest life which does not lack anything, an ideal life – according to your own imaginations – have you the picture of this ideal life before you? – Good. Begin living it! After some time it disappears. It is subject to time. No matter what type of life it is – Beethoven's life, Michelangelo's life – it does not matter, what kind of life it is – emperor's life, a life full of youthhood, sunshine and with a view to last for a thousand years – imagine such a life! Thousand years pass away quickly. And if you extend these thousand years, since it is a life in time and space – be it a life of time and space of this physical universe, or the time and space of the dream-world, or a time and space of a heavenly world, yet it is a life in time and space, and therefore, it has its opposites always ready at hand. Even when there is perfect harmony in this most perfect life you want to live and are living now, something in the soul is restless. You have got everything you want, yet something in the soul is restless. That is the fate of all types of life, no matter how glorious they are – therefore you never can have peace or happiness or real sunshine in your life, if you live outside ME, or the Seer in you, outside the Observer in you, the Infinite in you, the Absolute in you, the boundless Joy and Peace in you.

No matter what you are – a prophet – a son of God – you can imagine yourself to be a son of God – think like him, feel like him, pray like him, work like him – yet you will have no peace, real peace, unless you jump out of this role of a prophet's life into ME, into the Observer that I am in you, the Witness in all things, in all Beings, timeless and eternal.

You will make a mistake if you catch my body and bury it in the earth and think you have made an end of me. You have not touched me at all. Body is a small thing. Even the body of the greatest champion in the world, the world's best boxer is not too big a thing for a small stone. A small stone can kill him. No physical body, even that of a superman, can be indestructible, not even that of a Mystic or son of God. Physical body is only a cloth.

When it becomes old, or even when it is new, is all torn and useless, you just drop it. The outer conditions of the body exert no influence on the inner state, because I am not in the psychological being, emotional being, psychic being.

All your chakras are useless for me. I stand outside the chakras. I am unlimited. Chakras are limited. I am too subtle; chakras are gross, even if they create heavenly worlds.

This Being is the true God, the real Truth, the Eternal, the Absolute, the Immortal. Only a life in this is real Life. Outside this, even if it is the life of a God, it is attended with problems.

You know of Gods fighting. Fighting does not take place in ME. In ME is infinite Harmony. There is no want to fight with another. There is nothing to set in opposition with another. It is a unitary experience, it is a perfect experience, it is real divine Life.

This is the message of the Omkarananda-Upanishad.

Brahmavid Brahmaiva Bhavati

Brahmavid brahmaiva bhavati. The knower of the Brahman becomes the Brahman. Here knowing and being are one and the same. You not only know that you are infinite Consciousness-Bliss, but you become this infinite Consciousness-Bliss. To know Truth is to be the Truth. All Knowledge should and will ultimately lead to Knowledge of Brahman.

Pursue Knowledge passionately with all the love of your heart, the attention and concentration of your intelligence, with all the energies of your will. Knowledge builds character. Knowledge is power. Knowledge is light. Knowledge unfolds various abilities, capacities and brings you, when these abilities and capacities are put to use, immense wealth. Knowledge leads you to God-experience. The ultimate aim of every form of Knowledge is experience of the supreme Happiness, supreme Peace, infinite Knowledge, and supreme Perfection.

Obtain the highest Knowledge, the Knowledge of your inner Being as the ultimate Reality, the absolute Life, the source of all Perfections.

Gain a Knowledge that is all-independent, self-sustaining, all-perfect, unconditional and eternal. Guided by Wisdom all forms of Knowledge lead to the Knowledge of all Knowledges, the Supreme Knowledge. Brahmajñāna is Brahma-Anubhava, the Knower of Brahman becomes Brahman himself.

Paramahamsa Omkarananda Saraswati